Nothing to Prove

Nothing to Prove

∼O The Jim Abbott Story

by Bob Bernotas

KODANSHA INTERNATIONAL
New York • Tokyo • London

Kodansha America, Inc.
114 Fifth Avenue,
New York, New York 10011, U.S.A.

Kodansha International Ltd.
17-14 Otowa 1-chome,
Bunkyo-ku, Tokyo 112, Japan

Published in 1995 by Kodansha America, Inc.

Library of Congress Cataloging-in-Publication Data

Bernotas, Bob.
   Nothing to prove : the Jim Abbott story / by Bob Bernotas.
      p.   cm.
   Includes bibliographical references and index.
   ISBN 1-56836-064-9
   1. Abbott, Jim, 1967–   . 2. Baseball players—United States—
Biography. 3. Physically handicapped athletes—United States—
Biography. I. Title.
GV865.A26B47 1995
796.357092—dc20
[B]   95-6917

Book design by Laura Hough

Printed in the United States of America

95 96 97 98 99 RRD/H 10 9 8 7 6 5 4 3 2 1

To Carol

∼○ Contents

∼○ Acknowledgment

All thanks are due to John Urda, my editor at Kodansha America, who originally contacted me about doing this project, and managed it with a deft hand and light touch.

Nothing to Prove

I

∽○ No-Hitter

Dark clouds invaded the sky over Yankee Stadium on that early September Saturday afternoon. Pregame showers had held down the attendance. And so, even though the Yankees were locked in a tight divisional race with the defending world champion Toronto Blue Jays, a relatively small crowd of just 27,225 turned out for their game against Cleveland.

The subdued atmosphere in this barely half-filled ball-park posed a striking contrast to the scene there the previous night. Three years before, Manny Ramirez, a native of the upper Manhattan neighborhood of Washington Heights, had been hailed as New York City's top high school baseball player. He was selected by Cleveland in the first round of baseball's amateur draft and quickly developed into the gem of the club's minor-league farm system.

On Friday night, the 21-year-old prospect, called up from the minors a few days earlier, was playing in his second big-league game only minutes from where he grew up, where he learned to play baseball, where he used to root for the home team. The stadium in the South Bronx that he had gone to as a kid was packed with family and friends. Normally they were Yankees fans, but for this night they cheered for a visiting player, a neighborhood kid who had grown up and made them proud.

Ramirez did not disappoint them. He led Cleveland to victory, pounding out two home runs and driving a double off the left-field wall that nearly went out for a third round-tripper. It was the kind of story that would have seemed too corny for the movies, yet it really happened, and the TV and newspaper reporters made the most of it. But as the saying goes, tomorrow is another day. By Saturday afternoon, Ramirez's heroics would be old news.

That's how baseball is. You play 162 games every year, more if your team is fortunate enough to make it to the playoffs or the World Series. Each day tells another story, presenting another opportunity to succeed or fail. "This ain't a football game," Earl Weaver, the Baltimore Orioles' colorful former manager, used to remind overly enthusiastic reporters. "We do this every day." What happens on any given day passes overnight into memory, into history, as you turn your attention to the task at hand, the game—*today's* game.

So if yesterday belonged to Manny Ramirez, who would today belong to? Of course, no one could say. The Yankees' starting pitcher, Jim Abbott, hoped this might be his day. He arrived at the ballpark that morning wearing his lucky jeans, the ones that he marked with an X inside the waistband. The way things were going, he needed all the good-luck charms he could find.

After four years as the California Angels' most popular player, Abbott, suddenly and shockingly, was traded, shipped off the previous December to that athletic pressure cooker, New York City. The Yankees had not been a pennant contender for quite a few seasons. Their fans were frustrated; the owner was, as usual, impatient. The expectations of millions were pinned on this 25-year-old left-hander, along with the team's other off-season acquisitions. Abbott hit the big town full of confidence and hope, ready to consume the pressure and be nourished by it.

But as 1993 progressed, it looked like the pressure was consuming Abbott. All year long he struggled to put together strong outings back-to-back. Although he wasn't walking any more hitters than in past seasons, he had far fewer strikeouts than in his best years in California. In five months, with just one left to play, Abbott's earned run average was a mediocre 4.31, he had won only nine games and lost 11 and failed to win in five of his last six starts.

Abbott's last outing, in Cleveland six days earlier, was a disaster, his worst performance of the year so far. The Cleveland hitters pounded him for 10 hits and scored seven runs before the Yankees' manager, Buck Showalter, mercifully sent his wounded left-hander to a fourth-inning shower. But Abbott is an intensely driven athlete who takes losing very hard. Instead of hitting the showers he hit the streets of Cleveland and punished himself with a three-mile run.

While Abbott was gone, the Yankees rallied, climbed out of the 7-3 hole that he dug for them, and went on to win the game, 14-8. When Abbott returned to the visitors' clubhouse after his run, Showalter asked him, "Why'd you come back?" Abbott knew that his manager was ribbing him, with double-edged locker-room humor. Still, Abbott could not shake the feeling that the Yankees remained in the race despite his pitching rather than because of it. He had spent untold sleepless nights dwelling on that troubling thought.

And now, on this dreary, clammy late-summer after-noon, Abbott prepared to take the mound once more. The Yan-kees had lost three of their last four games and needed a win to stay close to the first-place Blue Jays. Obviously, a strong outing by Abbott would contribute to the cause and help salvage what, to this point, had been his most disappointing season in base-ball.

Analyzing his last start, Abbott felt that he hadn't chal-lenged the Cleveland hitters, that he had let the batters dictate his pitches. He resolved that this time he would pitch his own game. As Abbott warmed up, bullpen coach Mark Connor came over to him and suggested, "Let's work the outside of the plate more and mix in more breaking pitches." It was good advice: move the ball around the strike zone, keep the hitters guessing.

The game didn't start auspiciously for Abbott. He got behind on the first hitter, Kenny Lofton, and walked him on five pitches. But the second batter, Felix Fermin, grounded into a double play, and then Carlos Baerga flied out to left field. Ab-bott chugged off the mound, pumped up by the double play, re-lieved, if not exactly relaxed.

In the top of the second, Abbott struck out the first and last hitters and got another to fly out, so his one-out walk of Randy Milligan did no damage. He was settling into a comfort-able groove. After the first batter in the third inning flied out, Abbott retired the next five on infield grounders.

Meanwhile, the Yankees had taken the lead, 3-0. There's nothing like a three-run cushion and solid defensive play to help a pitcher find his confidence. For much of the sea-son Abbott had difficulty protecting leads, but not today. He walked Milligan again to lead off the fifth, but last night's hero, Manny Ramirez, hit into a double play to erase the runner. A fly ball to left retired the side. The sixth inning was equally routine—a line out, a walk, a fly out, and a ground out.

With just three innings to go, Cleveland still had gotten nothing close to a hit. *Nothing close to a hit?* By this time, Dewayne Staats, one of the Yankees' television announcers, had told his listeners to call their friends and neighbors. Jim Abbott of the New York Yankees, in his modest, unspectacular way, was now two-thirds of his way to pitching a no-hitter.

After every inning, Yankee catcher Matt Nokes sat next to his pitcher in the dugout. Nokes felt that, since Abbott had been struggling lately, it would help build up his confidence to review each successful inning right after it was over. But as the innings passed and the game grew late, Nokes suddenly stopped speaking to Abbott.

There is a custom in baseball, founded on equal parts superstition and good sense, that when a pitcher is throwing a no-hitter, nobody may talk to him about it. And to be on the safe side, it is considered wise not to talk to him about anything else.

Baseball players know that a no-hitter is something very rare. In their 91-year history, the New York Yankees have played well over 14,000 games. In only eight of them did a Yankees pitcher throw an official no-hitter, the last in 1983.

Consequently, no one wants to jinx a potential no-hitter by reminding the pitcher about it. After all, he's pitching the game, he knows better than anyone what is going on out there. And why bother him with useless advice? If he's pitching a no-hitter, then he certainly doesn't need any advice, does he? So once the no-hitter became a real possibility that afternoon, there was no more talk in the Yankees dugout within earshot of Jim Abbott.

But as soon as Abbott went back to the mound, the dugout came alive. Manager Buck Showalter weighed every deci-sion with extra care. "It puts more pressure on the manager and the coaches and the players," he observed. "You have to make sure you position your guys correctly [in the field] for their hit-ters. There's a lot of talk going on back and forth in the dugout." Then, once three outs were recorded, Abbott would return to his seat and everyone clammed up again.

At the same time, there was, through most of the game, an oddly muted feeling in the stadium. Maybe it was the omi-nous sky. Maybe it was the methodical way that Abbott was set-ting down the Cleveland hitters. Maybe, in light of the Yankees' recent slump, just winning the game would have been enough to satisfy the fans. But whatever the reason, there was little of the electricity that usually fills the stands when something unusual and important is happening on the diamond.

It took a brilliant defensive play to wake up the crowd. With one out in the seventh inning, Albert Belle, a .290 hitter on the season, smacked a shot into the hole between second and third base. Randy Velarde, the Yankees' third-string shortstop, broke to his right. Third baseman Wade Boggs broke to his left.

As a rookie coming up with the Boston Red Sox in 1982, Boggs was a terrific-hitting 24-year-old first baseman. But there was a problem: the Red Sox had an excellent defensive first baseman, Dave Stapleton, whom they did not want to take out of the lineup. Boggs might have been the team's designated hitter, but that slot was filled by all-time great Carl Yastrzemski, who was winding down his Hall of Fame career. The team's front office knew that Boggs had the potential to be a perennial .300-plus hitter. In order to get him into the everyday lineup, the Red Sox converted Boggs into a third baseman.

At first, Boggs struggled at his new position. Through persistence and hard work, fielding hundreds and thousands of ground balls during long practice sessions, Boggs made himself into a respectable, and eventually an excellent, defensive third baseman. Signed by the Yankees as a free agent after the 1992 season, his investment in defense paid a valuable dividend that September afternoon.

Boggs lunged toward the hole and made a diving stop of Belle's grounder. He went to his knees, gathered up the ball, and scrambled to his feet, throwing hard. First baseman Don Mattingly made the stretch, but the play was not even close. Belle was out easily and the crowd screamed. In a single moment everyone in the stadium suddenly seemed to realize that Boggs had saved Jim Abbott's no-hitter.

"Great play," declared Yankee coach Clete Boyer, a superb defensive third baseman in his day, after the game. "We had Wade shaded over toward third because Belle hits down the line. I told Wade," Boyer laughed, "he should have stayed on his knees [to make the throw]." Boggs, who insisted he wasn't thinking about saving a no-hitter at that moment, responded dryly, "I would never throw off my knees."

As the Yankees took the field in the top of the eighth inning, the crowd rose to their feet and remained standing for every pitch. No doubt about it, the fans who came to the stadium in spite of the threatening weather were being repaid for their dedication. Those unlucky folks who elected to stay home would be kicking themselves for days if Abbott managed to pull off a no-hitter.

Nobody even considered leaving early, nobody, that is, except for George Steinbrenner, the Yankees' controversial owner. It seems that he had a plane to catch. Rather than take a later flight, Steinbrenner walked out of the stadium as Abbott was attempting to write his name into Yankee history.

Abbott struck out Manny Ramirez, the hometown kid,

on a low pitch to lead off the eighth. Ramirez's backswing on the third strike hit catcher Nokes, who rolled in the dirt but held on to the ball. Abbott retired the next hitter on a ground ball and walked the following one. With two out and one on, pinch hitter Sandy Alomar bounced a grounder to third. Boggs short-hopped the ball and threw him out to end the inning.

Now, with one inning left to play, the Yankees were governed by two unspoken rules: don't talk to Jim Abbott and don't make any mistakes.

After the Yankees took the field for the top of the ninth, Showalter called the bullpen and coach Mark Connor answered the phone. "Send in Lee Smith," the manager told him, and immediately hung up. Just days earlier, the Yankees acquired the all-time save leader for their stretch drive.

Showalter turned to pitching coach Tony Cloninger and said, "Watch how quickly that phone rings." Of course, he'd have to be crazy to take out his starter in the ninth inning of a no-hitter. Within seconds Connor called back, screaming hysterically, which sent Showalter and Cloninger into a fit of laughter, relieving some of the tension that had filled the Yankees dugout.

But out on the field, shortstop Randy Velarde nearly was overcome with nervousness. He looked to his left and saw Mike Gallego at second and Don Mattingly at first bouncing up and down. Velarde tried to imitate them, but no matter how hard he tried to lift his feet, they just wouldn't move. "I said, 'Come on, feet!'" he recalled afterward. "It was funny. I didn't know how to act."

They didn't want to show it, for fear of jinxing their pitcher, but Abbott's teammates had become completely consumed by the no-hitter. "The last couple innings," Mattingly recalled, "I had huge goose bumps on my forearms, and the hair on the back of my neck was standing up."

"You try not to get caught up in it," second baseman Mike Gallego admitted, "but it's hard. You really have to continue to play the game. You're happy if you get the opportunity to keep it going for him."

The first batter, Kenny Lofton, attempted to break up the no-hitter by bunting his way on base, and the crowd, which had been on its feet for every pitch since the eighth inning, booed. Instead, Lofton hit a meek roller to second. Gallego got his chance to "keep it going" and fielded the ball cleanly, throwing Lofton out as the crowd roared.

The next Cleveland hitter, Felix Fermin, nearly broke the hearts of Abbott, his teammates, and the 27,225 fans when he blasted a long drive to deep left-center field. Fermin's hit seemed headed over the wall as speedy center fielder Bernie Williams raced toward the ball. "I didn't know if it was out [of the park]," he said later, "but I knew I had to move fast." Williams chased the fly all the way to the warning track, about 390 feet from home plate, and made the catch in front of the Yankees bullpen. Two out, and the crowd was going wild with anticipation.

Abbott, one out away from history, had to face Carlos Baerga, who was enjoying a superior season at the plate. His final 1993 totals—21 home runs, 114 runs batted in, and a .321 batting average—would be among the best ever posted by a second baseman. Earlier that season, he had hit three home runs in a single game. In other words, Baerga was not only Cleveland's best hitter, he was one of the toughest outs in the American League.

A switch-hitter, Baerga came to the plate batting left-handed. Normally, a left-handed batter is at a big disadvantage against a left-handed pitcher like Abbott. However, Baerga, hitting right-handed, had been jammed all too often by Abbott's slider, a pitch that runs in on right-handers. He thought that, by shifting to the other side of the plate, he would take away the lefty's most effective weapon and even the odds.

"You never want to get no-hit," Baerga noted after the game, explaining his strategy. "That was really on my mind in my last at bat. I just wanted to get a hit any way possible."

At his shortstop position, Velarde was still nervous, but he hoped Baerga would hit it to him. "You always want the ball in a situation like that," he reflected. "If you don't, it's going to find you anyway."

The noise in Yankee Stadium was so loud that Velarde was unable to hear the ball coming off Baerga's bat. The softly hit grounder was heading toward him, but ever so slowly. "I really wanted the ball to come my way," the shortstop maintained, "but I wanted it to be hit hard." At least he was able to get his feet unstuck.

Velarde charged forward, scooped up the grounder, and threw to Mattingly, retiring Baerga for the final out of the game. As the ball hit Mattingly's mitt, Abbott threw open his arms and shouted, "How about that, baby!" Showalter, who seldom shows any emotion at all, jumped off the bench and nearly hit his head on the dugout ceiling. Abbott had pitched a no-hitter in the heat of a September pennant race against a lineup that included six players hitting .298 or better. "This was Jim Abbott's day," Baerga said with resignation afterward.

"I'm thrilled to come out of that last start and pitch a game like this," Abbott told reporters in the locker room after the cheering died down and he took his final bows to the fans. "It makes it doubly nice being in September and being in a pennant race." The 4-0 victory moved the Yankees just one game behind the league-leading Toronto Blue Jays.

But, the typically modest pitcher added, "I think no-hitters take a little bit of luck." Abbott recalled that earlier that same season, on May 29, he had held the Chicago White Sox hitless for seven and one-third innings, before Bo Jackson broke it up with a single. If not for the fielding exploits of Boggs in the seventh and Williams in the ninth, this no-hitter might have been just another strong start. The way things had been going for Abbott in 1993, he would have been satisfied with that.

In fact, Abbott didn't feel that he had pitched that poorly in his disastrous outing six days earlier. "To be honest," he maintained, "I can hardly tell you the difference—other than a little more command on my breaking ball—between this start and the last one."

Frankly, Abbott's game was nothing like the dominating, no-hit masterpieces thrown by power pitchers like Bob Feller, Sandy Koufax, or Nolan Ryan. He struck out only three batters and walked five. On the whole, his performance was more workmanlike than artistic. Still, Abbott did not allow a runner past first base, and twice he erased potential threats by getting the next batter to ground into a double play. So that big zero under the H on the scoreboard was all that anyone really needed to know.

And this Cleveland lineup was filled with strong hitters, as David Letterman pointed out when Abbott appeared on his late-night television program a few days later. "This isn't the Mets we're talking about here," the comedian observed as Abbott laughed. "This was a legitimate major-league team."

Once the postgame interviews were finished, Abbott showered, dressed, and headed home with two bottles of champagne. He and his wife, Dana, met team captain Mattingly for a celebration dinner at an Upper East Side restaurant. After dinner, as Jim and Dana Abbott walked back to their nearby apartment, people kept stopping him on the street to autograph early editions of the Sunday newspapers.

Once they got home, the Abbotts discovered that their answering machine was filled with messages from both friends and strangers phoning to offer their congratulations. The Baseball Hall of Fame in Cooperstown, New York, also had called, asking Abbott whether he would send the hat that he wore and the baseball he used to retire Baerga for the final out of the game.

On Sunday, the Yankee Stadium grounds crew presented Abbott with the pitching rubber from his no-hitter, signed by all his teammates. Naturally Abbott was honored, but the fresh rubber on the mound announced that there was another game to play. The Yankees were battling for first place and the no-hitter counted no more in the standings than any other win. Abbott knew that this was no time to bask in the glow of yesterday's heroics. As he said before his next start, "I have to act like it never happened."

Still, there was no denying that Abbott had achieved something unique. From 1901, the year the American League was founded, to 1993, approximately 140,000 major-league baseball games were played. Only 216 of them were no-hitters, an infinitesimally small .15 percent. But Abbott's achievement was even rarer than that.

"If you took every no-hitter ever thrown in the big leagues," sports writer Tom Verducci mused in *Sports Illustrated,* "and arranged them in alphabetical order by pitcher, the one thrown . . . by James Anthony Abbott would be at the top. Should you delineate the no-hitters according to their inspirational value, the same one would lead the list."

It was true—his was like no other no-hitter thrown in this century, for Jim Abbott of the New York Yankees had been born without a right hand. Nevertheless, he became a schoolboy marvel, a college star, an Olympic hero, and now, in his fifth big-league season, he was pitching for a pennant contender.

Throughout his career, Abbott always insisted that, despite his apparent disability, he was the same as any other pitcher. But that would no longer be true because, on September 4, 1993, Jim Abbott accomplished with one hand what only a tiny number of major-league pitchers had done with two. He had pitched a no-hitter.

2

∼○ Dreams

"**G**rowing up, I always pictured myself as a baseball player," Jim Abbott once told a reporter for *Time* magazine, "but I can't remember how many hands I had in my dreams."

James Anthony Abbott was born on September 19, 1967, in Flint, Michigan, a small industrial city of approximately 150,000 residents, about 50 miles north of Detroit. His parents, Mike and Kathy Abbott, were both 18 years old at the time and just out of high school.

It's never easy to have a child at such a young age. What made things doubly difficult for Kathy and Mike Abbott was that their baby had been born without a right hand. When a child is born with a disability, there are the inevitable questions: Why us? How could this happen? But after the initial shock and disappointment, the most important thing the parents must ask themselves is, What do we do now? The Abbotts set their minds to making the best, most "normal" life that they could for their son, Jim.

Reflecting on his childhood, Jim Abbott marveled at the challenges that his parents faced and the remarkable job they did handling them. "They were young," he explained. "They were alone. There were no support groups. Really, I look back with admiration."

Getting by was a struggle for the Abbotts in those early years. Jim's father packed meat and sold cars. His mother studied at home. In time, both parents finished college. Today, Mike Abbott works as a sales manager for the Anheuser-Busch brewing company. Kathy Abbott, after having been a teacher, went to law school and is now an attorney with a firm that specializes in education law.

The Abbotts did their best to treat Jim the same as any other child, raising him "by instinct," as Kathy Abbott once said. "All we did is let him do what he wanted," she insisted. When Jim was ready to begin school, a doctor fitted him with an artificial right hand, a fiberglass-and-metal prosthesis. Jim called it a "hook."

"The doctor told us if he didn't have it," Kathy Abbott recalled, "he wouldn't be able to do things like tie his shoes and use scissors." But Jim hated the device. It frightened some of the other children and drew even more attention to his condition. "He was self-conscious about it," his mother continued. "We told him it was the best thing for him, but we finally gave up and quit making him wear it." He never wore the mechanical hand again.

Jim's parents always told him that he could do whatever he wanted. When, like many kids, he became interested in sports, they tried to come up with a way to accommodate him. They bought Jim a soccer ball, figuring that a sport that did not allow the use of one's hands was best suited to his condition. The only problem was, despite his parents' best intentions, Jim didn't like soccer.

Maybe Jim thought that, by taking up soccer, he would be giving in to his disability. But perhaps the explanation is even simpler. After all, every kid in the neighborhood was playing baseball, not soccer, and naturally Jim wanted to join their games. Whatever the reason, his mother laughed, "The only sport Jim didn't need his hand for is about the only one he hasn't gravitated to." And as if to confound these well-meaning parents even further, Jim's younger brother, Chad, who has both hands, became the soccer player in the family.

But it wasn't easy, at first, for this would-be athlete. One time, the other kids chose up sides for a game and he wasn't picked. Jim was only five, but he knew why he was left out. He ran home, in tears, and told his mother and father what had happened.

Like any parents, Mike and Kathy Abbott's first impulse was to console their child. They wanted to hug him sympathetically, shield him from the hurt, tell him that everything was going to be all right. Instead, they did something much harder. They insisted that Jim go back outside and tell the others that he wanted to play.

"When I was little, my parents always encouraged me to be outgoing," Abbott has noted with gratitude. "My dad was always pushing me, when I'd see someone new, to walk up to the kid, shake his hand and say, 'Hi, my name is Jim Abbott.'" When they moved into a new neighborhood, Kathy and Mike Abbott coaxed their son to go around and meet the kids and ask to play their games.

But because Jim had a special condition he had to develop special skills. In short, he had to learn how to throw and
catch a baseball with just his left hand. So, Mike Abbott came
up with the now famous "glove-hand switch" that has as-
tounded onlookers wherever his son has played, from Little
League to the major leagues. To Jim, however, it's no big deal.
"Everyone has limitations," he had said, casually. "It's just that
mine are different from most people's. So I learned to do things
differently."

Here's how the glove-hand switch works: Abbott
throws the ball with his left hand while balancing a right-
handed fielder's glove on the end of his right arm. After the ball
is released, he slips his left hand into the glove and gets himself
in position to receive the ball as it is thrown or hit back to him.
Having caught the ball, Abbott cradles the glove in the crook of
his right arm and, resting it against his chest, removes the glove
from his hand. He now can take the ball out of the glove and
throw it again, repeating the whole process.

On paper, this may seem complicated, but Jim was an
eager pupil and he spent hours practicing the move, playing
countless games of catch with his father. He also would throw a
rubber ball against a brick wall outside his family's townhouse,
pitching imaginary games against big-league stars. It was not
only fun, it was what Jim had to do if he was ever going to play
ball with the other kids.

Jim began throwing harder and harder and gradually
moving closer to the wall. As the ball caromed back to him
ever more quickly, he learned to make the hand-glove switch
with astonishing speed. He became so smooth and fluid—so
natural—at the move that, in time, many observers, even professional baseball people, had difficulty detecting it.

Since there are no designated hitters in playground ballgames, Jim also had to learn how to handle a baseball bat. He would simply hold the bat with his left hand, balance the handle on the end of his right arm, and swing with all his might. More often than not, his combination of strength, reflexes, and hand-eye coordination would connect for a hit.

Now the neighborhood kids no longer had any reason not to welcome Jim into their games. The outgoing youngster soon became "one of the guys." "I still have friends that I've had since the fourth grade," he likes to say with pride. "Right away, they accepted me and I accepted them." And sports, especially baseball, was the main avenue of acceptance.

Like most kids, Jim and his pals played ball all day and might have done it all night, if they could have gotten away with it. Sometimes, they would pitch a tennis or Whiffle ball at their makeshift backstop, a lawn chair. (No kid ever wants to be the catcher.) Depending on how far you hit the ball into Jim's big backyard, it would count as a single, double, triple, or, if it went into the trees, a home run.

When Jim was 11 years old, he told his parents that he wanted to play Little League baseball, because, he recalled years later, "that's what kids did in Flint, Michigan. . . . People were supportive. There were always skeptics, but they kept it to themselves."

When Jim arrived at his first practice, his coach asked him what position he wanted to play, and without hesitation Jim replied, "Pitcher." The boy's confidence would have impressed even the most skeptical coach, so Jim got the chance to prove what he could do on the mound. In his first start for his team, Lydia Simon Real Estate, Jim pitched a five-inning no-hitter.

He quickly became known as one of the best Little League pitchers in town. When he was 12, a reporter from the

Flint Journal called Jim's house, asking to interview him. Jim's parents were taken by surprise. "We hadn't been paying much attention to what he was doing," Kathy Abbott admitted. "We just knew he was playing at the neighborhood fields and wasn't getting into any mischief."

By the time Jim was in junior high school, word of his pitching feats caught the ear of the baseball coach at Flint Central High School, Bob Holec. Holec was eager to see this local phenom in action, especially since Jim would be attending Flint Central the following school year. He got his chance when Jim pitched in the city junior championship game.

Naturally Holec was impressed with Jim's 80-mile-an-hour fastball. But the coach also had his doubts. "I was just as curious as anybody else," Holec recounted. "I wondered if he could handle balls hit back to him. I was talking to his father when a kid hit a high-hopper back to the mound. Jimmy threw him out. His father and I looked at each other, and I said, 'I guess that answers that.' "

As a ninth grader at Flint Central, Jim played for the junior varsity team. The next year he pitched for Holec's varsity squad and played left field on the days when he wasn't on the mound. One time, the opposing coach decided to test what he thought would be Jim's Achilles' heel, his fielding. He instructed eight consecutive batters to bunt the ball right back toward Jim, a difficult play even for a two-handed pitcher.

The most effective way to field a softly bunted ball is to pick it up with the bare hand and throw to first base in a single, fluid motion. But Jim, immediately after pitching the ball, would have transferred his glove from his right arm to his left hand, in case the ball was hit back sharply to him. And so, he would need to toss off his glove before he could scoop up the ball and attempt the throw.

The first of those eight hitters reached base safely. Jim then threw out each of the next seven. "If they think they can bunt on me," Abbott has said with typical confidence, "let them bunt on me. After I throw enough of them out, they usually figure out that they'd better try something else." After that day, opponents had to look for other weaknesses in Jim Abbott's game to exploit. They seldom found any.

For the next three years, Bob Holec was not just Jim's varsity baseball coach; he also became one of the pitcher's biggest fans. Nearly two years after Jim graduated, Holec told *Sports Illustrated* that Jim's high school days had given him some of his fondest baseball memories, reciting some of them for the reporter.

Holec recalled the game when Jim, playing left field, made a running catch of a fly ball and then unleashed a 270-foot throw to nail a runner at the plate. Then there was the time he hit a 330-foot game-winning home run to center field. And he couldn't forget the day when, after a poor outing in the first game of a doubleheader, Jim paused to talk with a handicapped kid and then came back to win the nightcap in extra innings with a three-run homer.

Jim was an astounding all-around ballplayer. Besides his pitching and left-field duties, he also played some first base and even handled one inning at shortstop. (Of course, the only thing rarer than a left-handed shortstop is a one-handed shortstop, and Jim was both.) His hitting was equally phenomenal. In his senior year, Jim batted cleanup and hit for a .427 average, leading the team with seven home runs and 36 runs batted in.

But his pitching deserved most of the attention. As a senior, Jim won 10 games and lost only three, and he posted an incredibly low 0.76 earned run average. In 73 innings pitched, he struck out 148 batters—an average of two per inning—and gave up just 16 hits. In other words, Jim was virtually unhittable. He even threw four no-hitters that season, including a perfect game in which only two balls were hit in fair territory.

Jim also spent three summers pitching for the Flint Grossi team in the local Connie Mack League. Although he was just 15 when he joined the club, Jim's determination, outgoing manner, and overpowering fastball immediately won over his 17- and 18-year-old teammates. "When Jim pitched," Flint Grossi's coach, Ted Mahan, recalled, "they got a little more ex- cited because they wanted to do a little better for Jim. In the three years I had him he . . . lost so many tight games. I think our guys got maybe too hyped up. He lost so many games 2-1, 1-0. . . . But he won a lot of big ones, too." Jim also won his first taste of national acclaim when NBC's *George Michael Sports Machine* broadcast a feature on him.

During Jim's junior year, Flint Central's football team was thin at the quarterback position. Holec, who was also an assistant football coach, managed to talk his star pitcher into trying out for the team. As the backup quarterback, Jim spent most of that season learning how to handle the snap from the center. In time, he developed a technique that was every bit as fluid as his glove-hand switch.

As the center snapped the football, Jim would position his left hand underneath the ball and his right arm on top. Then, he would bring the ball up to his chest and get a firm grip on the laces. Now he was ready either to throw a pass or to hand the ball off to a running back.

In his senior year, Jim started the last three games of the season at quarterback and passed for 600 yards with six touch- downs, including four in a state semifinal game. "I honestly feel he is good enough as an athlete," insisted his high school foot- ball coach, Joe Eufinger, "that if his first love was football, he could have been a quarterback at the college level." His football prowess was the subject of a feature on NBC's *The NFL Today* pregame show.

Jim was also a terrific punter, averaging 37.5 yards per kick in his senior year. A natural athlete if there ever was one, he was proficient at basketball, as well. Playing forward, Jim led Flint Central's intramural basketball league in scoring.

After his spectacular senior baseball season, Jim was faced with a big decision. In June 1985, as he was about to graduate high school, Jim was chosen by the Toronto Blue Jays in the 36th and final round of baseball's annual amateur draft. The Blue Jays offered him a $50,000 bonus if he would sign with the team. "We felt, even at the time," Toronto general manager Pat Gillick said, more than three years later, "that he had the ability to overcome his handicap."

It was for Jim more than a thrill to be selected by a major-league club. It was literally a dream come true. "I've grown up daydreaming about pitching in the majors, just like any kid might," he recalled the following year. "I can imagine myself pitching in a starting rotation with Orel Hershiser and Fernando Valenzuela. You know, 'Now starting for the Los Angeles Dodgers, Jim Abbott.'" Being drafted convinced him it was possible.

"The Blue Jays say they didn't take me because I was special," he insisted at the time. "They took me because they think I can pitch in the majors. I think I can too. It won't be easy, but it's possible. I'm not handicapped. I'm just a pitcher, same as anybody else. Better than some, not as good as others."

But Jim had to face some hard facts. Good left-handed pitching is one of the most valuable and sought-after commodities in baseball. Nevertheless, he was not picked until the last round of the draft. The top high school and college prospects had been scooped up in the early rounds, and hundreds more players were chosen before Toronto got around to calling his name. The Blue Jays may have thought that this 17-year-old pitcher had a shot, but it was a long shot.

In fact, Jim had not been heavily recruited even by the top college baseball programs. Perhaps there was some apprehension over his disability, but that was not the only reason. College coaches want hard throwers who can fire fastballs at speeds of more than 90 miles per hour. However, Jim's fastball, at the time, was clocked in only the low to mid-80s, and that was his only pitch. And so, Jim's parents knew that he would have to be realistic about the future.

"We've been very cautious," Kathy Abbott explained. "We've tried to instill in him that he's got to think beyond baseball and get his education. I don't think that he's ever been overconfident that he's going to make it to the majors." *Overconfident?* Maybe not. Still, Mike and Kathy Abbott always told Jim that he could do anything he wanted. And there were those dreams.

Suddenly, a solution presented itself. One major-college baseball coach, the University of Michigan's Bud Middaugh, was very interested in adding Jim to his team. "I wouldn't have recruited him," Middaugh insisted, "if I hadn't felt like he could play here." And Jim was eager to play at Michigan, for many reasons.

He was a fan of the university's football team, a perennial Big Ten Conference power. One of his boyhood idols, Flint native Rich Leach, had been a two-sport star at Michigan. (Leach went on to play baseball for the Toronto Blue Jays.) The Michigan campus in Ann Arbor was not far from his hometown, so his parents could watch him play. And college ball would allow Jim the chance to improve his speed and develop a wider repertory of pitches without the added day-to-day pressure of professional competition.

And so, Jim chose the University of Michigan over the Toronto Blue Jays. "I always felt I could make it to the majors,' he maintained. "But I still had a lot to prove to a lot of people, including myself. And if it turned out that I was wrong in my estimate of my ability, then at least I would have gained a college education in the process."

Even if he never made it to the majors, the first 18 years of Jim Abbott's life were indisputable proof that "disability" does not have to mean "inability." OK, so Jim Abbott has only one hand. So what?

Nobody pitied him for it, nobody discouraged him because of it, nobody made a big fuss over it. "Not only my mom and dad," Abbott recalled, "but my teammates, teachers, classmates, friends, coaches, everybody . . . almost to the point of just *ignoring* it. I never heard anything about it. If anything at all came along that I couldn't handle, all anybody wanted to do was help."

But Mike Abbott gives the lion's share of the credit to his son. "I never heard Jim ask, 'Why me?' " his father has commented. "And as he grew up, I watched the way he handled himself around people. He's always had a lot of friends, always laughed. Even when some people said insensitive or cruel things. . . . I don't understand how he does it. His dad is now taking lessons from him." There may be no greater compliment that a parent can pay a child.

3

∼o College Star, Olympic Hero

The college baseball season starts in March, a full month earlier than in the major leagues, and is relatively brief, lasting between 55 and 65 games or so. But winter is an inconsiderate guest in Ann Arbor, Michigan, and usually overstays its welcome. To escape the biting chill of early March—and the unforgettable, finger-numbing sting created when an aluminum bat connects with an inside fastball in 40-degree air—the University of Michigan, like most northern colleges, plays much of its early schedule in the South.

The Michigan Wolverines began their 1986 season against Villanova University in a tournament in Orlando, Florida, with freshman Jim Abbott on the mound. The game began at 11:00 in the morning, and only a sparse crowd turned out for it. Still, an NBC camera crew was there to cover the college debut of the one-handed sensation from Flint.

It would be nice to report that Abbott dominated the opposing hitters, mowing them down one after another, grinning with satisfaction from the mound as batter upon batter slinked back to the bench, confounded by his overpowering stuff. But that isn't what happened.

In fact, Abbott pitched terribly. He loaded the bases in the first inning, but managed to work out of the jam with no runs allowed. In the second inning Abbott was even worse, yielding three singles and a walk before he had to leave the game. Despite his poor performance, Michigan went on to win, 8-4, and Abbott was embarrassed when, after the game, the rest of the team had to wait for him while he was interviewed for television.

His next outing, against the University of North Carolina, was no better. As the NBC cameras rolled, Abbott walked the first three hitters. He got the next batter to hit into a double play and picked off a runner to get out of the inning unscathed. When he struck out the leadoff hitter in the second inning, it appeared as if Abbott really would live up to his reputation. But then he gave up a walk followed by a two-run homer. Rattled, Abbott walked the next three batters and had to be taken out of the game. Michigan rallied and won, 17-8, but once again with no help from their famous freshman.

Michigan coach Bud Middaugh chalked up Abbott's wildness to a simple case of nerves. "There's so much attention on him every time he pitches," Middaugh insisted, "it'll take him a while to settle down." He decided that the best way to take some of the pressure off Abbott would be to give his freshman pitcher some appearances in relief.

A few days later, Michigan played North Carolina again. Down 3-2 in the seventh inning, with runners on first

and third and two out, Middaugh sent for Abbott. This time
responded well to the pressure and quickly pitched the t
North Carolina batter into a one-ball, two-strike hole.

Then suddenly, as the Wolverine catcher lobbed th
ball back to the mound, the runner on third took off and headed
for the plate. The steal of home may be the most exciting play in
baseball. It requires speed, daring, and split-second timing, and
the risk of failure is enormous. Obviously, it takes far less time to
throw a ball 60 feet, six inches, than it does to run 90 feet, so the
runner must catch the pitcher off guard and hope that the throw
home will be slow or, even better, wild. More than likely, the
North Carolina coach was hoping that Abbott's glove-hand
switch would delay his throw and even up the odds.

But Abbott was alert and unfazed. He caught the toss
from his catcher, removed the glove from his left hand, grabbed
the ball, and fired home. The runner was out by at least 20 feet
and the inning was over. "If they had done that on any of my
other pitchers," Middaugh recalled a year later, "they might
have got away with it. But Jim's much more aware." Michigan
went ahead in the eighth inning and Abbott chalked up his first
college victory, 6-3.

Abbott was still in the bullpen when the Wolverines
played their home opener against Grand Valley State. Senior
Scott Kamieniecki started the game, Abbott relieved him in the
fourth inning, and when it was over, the two future New York
Yankees teammates had combined to pitch a no-hitter. Middaugh decided that Abbott now was ready to become a starting
pitcher.

In his first start after rejoining the Michigan rotation,
Abbott was pounded by the University of Miami (Ohio), but
the Wolverines eventually went on to win the game, 6-5. Abbott rebounded from the poor outing and, next time out, tossed

a three-hit, 1-0 shutout against Western Michigan for his second win of the year. By this time, Abbott was attracting nationwide attention, more for his "human interest" story than for his pitching. He appeared on *Good Morning America* and *The Phil Donohue Show*, and during March, the ESPN network named him its Owens-Corning Amateur Athlete of the Week.

Over the course of the season, Abbott showed himself to be a capable freshman pitcher. Quick to learn, he enjoyed modest success, finishing the regular season with a 5-2 won-loss record. Michigan closed their schedule at 44-10 overall and went 13-3 within the Big Ten Conference, first place in the conference's Eastern Division.

The Wolverines beat Wisconsin and Minnesota in the first two rounds of the Big Ten postseason playoffs and had to face Minnesota in a rematch for the conference championship. Michigan fell behind early in the title game, so Middaugh brought Abbott in from the bullpen in the third inning. Abbott held the fort, striking out 10 batters and not allowing a hit until the eighth. Meanwhile, Michigan battled back to win the game, and the Big Ten championship, by a score of 9-5. Abbott got the victory and, for his strong relief effort, was named to the all-tournament team.

Abbott completed his first year of college ball with a 6-2 record and a respectable, if unspectacular, 4.11 ERA. A budding "power pitcher," he struck out 44 batters in 50⅓ innings. The following January, the Philadelphia Sports Writers Association chose Abbott as their "Most Courageous Athlete of the Year."

After losing his first start of the 1987 college season, 8-0, to Oklahoma, Abbott got hot and ran off a string of nine straight victories. During that stretch, he pitched 35 consecutive innings without giving up an earned run and notched two shutouts and a one-hitter. With Abbott as their ace, the Michigan Wolverines finished first in the Big Ten's Eastern Division, successfully defended their conference championship, and went on to the Northeast Regionals of the NCAA National College Baseball Tournament.

The tournament employs a double-elimination format—lose twice, and your team is out of the competition. The Wolverines dropped their first game and were on the verge of being sent home, so Middaugh called on his sophomore star to face Rider College. Five days earlier, in the Big Ten semifinal game, Abbott had pitched seven innings of six-hit ball against Purdue, and Middaugh was concerned that Abbott might be tired.

All the coach wanted was for Abbott to keep his team in the game and work as many strong innings as he could against Rider. Instead, he pitched a complete-game shutout—his third of the season—and Michigan breezed to a 10-0 win. "I was amazed that he was able to go the distance," Middaugh remarked afterward. Abbott scattered eight hits (including only one extra-base hit) and allowed just two Rider runners to reach third base, none after the third inning. Unfortunately, the Wolverines lost their next game and were eliminated from the tournament.

In all, Abbott led his team with 11 victories against only three losses and his ERA was a brilliant 2.08. He struck out 60, walked 39, and yielded 71 hits in 86⅓ innings, good numbers for a still-unpolished 19-year-old pitcher. Abbott's superb postseason performance earned him third-team All-America honors and attracted the attention of major-league scouts.

Of course, the scouts focused on his disability. That, after all, is their job, to determine a player's strengths and weaknesses and to evaluate how he maximizes the former and minimizes the latter. Plenty of young prospects have "all the tools," as the cliché goes, and never learn how to use them. Others may not possess the strongest arms, the greatest speed, or the most power, but, by compensating for their shortcomings and working with what they do have, can enjoy long big-league careers.

The scouts examined Abbott closely and liked what they saw. "After the second inning," observed Ed Katalinas of the Detroit Tigers, "there is no handicap." Bob Gardner of the California Angels was similarly impressed. "What amazes me is how he fields," the scout noted. "He has the tools to pitch in the majors." And Abbott scored highly on the checklist of San Diego Padres' scout, Steve Boros: "Good stuff. Live fastball. Decent curve. Throws strikes. If he stays healthy, he'll be a legitimate draft choice."

As summer approached, Abbott tried out for a spot on the United States's national amateur baseball team, Team USA. At first, Team USA's coach, Ron Fraser of the University of Miami, had all the usual doubts, but he quickly came around and added Abbott to his squad. "If you see him pitch a lot," Fraser noted, echoing what so many coaches, scouts, and fans were saying, "you don't even notice the hand."

To get in shape for the Pan American Games, which would be held that August in Indianapolis, Team USA embarked on a 34-game exhibition schedule. They won three out of four games against Japan's strong national team. Then, in mid-July, the tour took them to Cuba for a five-game series against the powerful Cuban national team, a dominant force in international baseball. The American press painted this U.S.-Cuba series as if it were a big rivalry, but Abbott knew better. "They are the best amateur team in the world," he said realistically, "and we're trying to get our respect back."

Abbott was scheduled to pitch the third game of the series in Havana. Cuba's baseball fans are among the most de-

voted and knowledgeable in the world. They knew all about
Abbott and his remarkable story and followed him everywhere,
through the streets, along the beaches. Most of all, the Cubans
were eager to see what the one-handed marvel could do against
their national heroes.

When Abbott took the mound in the first inning, the
crowd of more than 50,000 gave him a standing ovation. Cuba's
leadoff hitter, Victor Mesa, chopped a grounder down the third-
base line, 20 feet into the air. Abbott plucked the ball from the
air barehanded, fired to first, and threw Mesa out. "It was a
bang-bang play," he recounted. "I guess the crowd cheered for
four or five minutes. That broke the ice."

It was quite a display, and Abbott certainly deserved the
ovation. Still, Fraser was not sure what to make of the crowd's
reaction. "I don't think they took him seriously," the coach
maintained. "They looked at him as a handicapped guy." Fraser
wanted the Cuban fans to see and respect Abbott the way that
he did—as a pitcher, not as a curiosity.

Respect came a few innings later. Abbott held the
Cuban hitters in check and won the game, 8-3, becoming the
first American pitcher in almost 30 years to defeat the Cuban
team in Cuba. (Gregg Olson also won the fifth and final game of
the series for Team USA.) This time, Fraser was satisfied: the
50,000 Cuban fans were cheering Abbott for his pitching. "Abbott's a national hero down there," the coach said the following
month. "They'll be talking about him 20 years from now."

After the game, Abbott was congratulated by Cuba's
number-one baseball fan. "It was a great honor to shake hands
with Fidel Castro," the awe-struck pitcher recalled, "a man with
his physical presence and his place in history." One wag asked
him to compare the Cuban leader with Michigan's formidable
football coach, Bo Schembechler, and Abbott took the bait.

"They've both got a sort of tough guy, dictatorial presence about them," he responded innocently. There is no record of what the imperious Schembechler thought of Abbott's comparison, if he ever found out about it.

Abbott finished the tune-up tour with a 6-1 record and arrived at the Pan American Games in August as Team USA's most reliable starter. More than 6,000 athletes from 38 North, Central, and South American nations came to compete in 27 different sports. When the opening ceremonies were held in the famed Indianapolis Motor Speedway, Abbott, to his surprise, learned that he had been chosen among the 677 American athletes to lead the delegation and carry the flag in the parade of nations. Other finalists who were considered for the honor included world-champion diver Greg Louganis and basketball star David Robinson.

Team USA opened the round-robin tournament with back-to-back wins over Canada, 10-6, and Venezuela, 14-7. Abbott was scheduled to start the third game, against Nicaragua, and before he ever stepped on the mound, his team jumped out to a first-inning, 10-0 lead. "I was really anxious to get out there and throw the first pitch," he said later. "But I just sat there and waited and waited and waited."

When Abbott finally got to work in the bottom of the first, Nicaragua's leadoff hitter bunted to the left side of the infield, forcing the pitcher to try to make the play. There was not enough time for the glove-hand switch, of course, so he fielded the bunt barehanded and threw the batter out by two steps. Afterward someone suggested that bunting seemed like a less than sporting thing to do, but Abbott disagreed.

"The way I look at it," he replied, with an appealing cockiness, "if a batter is weak on an inside pitch, I'll throw inside. If they feel I'm a weak fielder, then they should try to take advantage of me. I think of it as an easy out." The Nicaraguan hitters learned their lesson and did not try to bunt on Abbott again.

The "mercy rule" is amateur baseball's version of the technical knockout. Any team that is leading by 10 or more runs after seven innings is simply declared the winner, game over. Since Team USA had amassed an 18-0 lead by that point, the carnage was called to a halt. Abbott had pitched the first five innings, allowed four hits and four walks and struck out six, and was awarded the victory.

The mercy rule also was invoked in Team USA's next game, a 14-1 rout of the team from the Netherlands Antilles. The following day, the United States defeated Cuba, 6-4, in a major upset. Before that game, Cuba had amassed a streak of 33 straight wins in Pan American Games competition. They had not lost at the Pan Am Games since 1967, the only time that the United States beat them out for the gold medal.

Thanks again to the mercy rule, Team USA was able to dispatch Aruba, 15-2, after just seven innings. Abbott worked three innings in the game, allowing no runs. The next day, however, they needed 11 innings to defeat Puerto Rico in the final round-robin game, 4-0. The United States finished the first leg of the tournament in first place and entered the medal round with a perfect 7-0 record. They would face Canada in the semi-finals.

Team USA got out to an early lead, but Canada tied it 5-5 in the third inning, so Abbott was called in from the bull-pen. He worked four and two-thirds innings and held Canada to three hits and one unearned run. Meanwhile, his teammates moved out in front and held on to win, 7-6, giving Abbott his second victory of the tournament. The win assured Team USA of no worse than a second-place finish at the Pan American

Games and also clinched a berth for the United States in the 1988 Summer Olympics.

In its semifinal game, Cuba rallied from a 5-1 deficit and beat Puerto Rico, 6-5, to earn a rematch against Team USA in the gold-medal game. It was an exciting, seesaw battle, but Cuba prevailed, 13-9, winning its seventh Pan American championship. Abbott and his teammates had to be satisfied with silver.

In three Pan Am appearances, Abbott won two games and allowed no earned runs. Over the entire summer, he won eight and lost one, with a 1.70 ERA, and struck out 51 batters in 48⅔ innings, walking just 18. Naturally, major-league scouts had attended the Pan Am Games and, as before, were enthusiastic about Abbott's prospects.

"The general public watches him because of his right arm," said Terry Ryan from the Minnesota Twins' organization, for example, "but the scouting people are interested in him because of the arm he throws with. . . . He has good velocity and a good curve. He's a good athlete, real strong and agile."

The Dodgers' Glenn Van Proyen sounded a mildly cautious note, claiming, "The one thing you worry about is a line drive going right at his head." But Abbott had an answer for that: "I just duck." And so do most two-handed pitchers, at least those who would like to live to a ripe old age.

Although he had dealt with reporters and interviewers before, the Pan American Games gave Abbott his first taste of sustained, intensive press attention. The more successful he was, the more they persisted in asking the inevitable, inescapable question: "How do you do it? How do you play baseball with just one hand?" To Abbott, of course, it was all second nature. "I don't even think about it," he finally told the press, with a touch of exasperation, "until you guys come around to remind me."

In October, the United States Baseball Federation honored Abbott with its annual Golden Spikes Award, recognizing him as the outstanding amateur baseball player of 1987. The award, according to the USBF, is based on "athletic ability, sportsmanship, character, and overall contribution to the sport," not strictly on performance. "I was sort of shocked," Abbott claimed after he was presented with the honor. "It's a very similar feeling to being told, 'You're going to carry the flag for the U.S. delegation [at the Pan American Games].' I can't believe I won it."

Having won the Golden Spikes, Abbott became a finalist for an even greater prize, the Amateur Athletic Union's Sullivan Award, which is presented every March to the previous year's top amateur athlete. The odds, however, were against him because, as always, the competition was stiff. The other Sullivan finalists that year included David Robinson, the nation's top college basketball player, world champions like swimmer Janet Evans and hurdler Greg Foster, and volleyball sensation Karch Kiraly. In addition, history was not on Abbott's side. Never in its 57 years had the Sullivan Award gone to a baseball player.

On March 7, 1988, Abbott and the other Sullivan Award finalists gathered at the Indianapolis Convention Center for the announcement of the award. "I had no business being invited to that dinner," he declared a few months later. "I thought Karch Kiraly . . . would win it." Abbott was shocked when his name was called and track star Jackie Joyner-Kersee, the 1987 Sullivan Award winner, presented him with the trophy. "It's just incredible," he exclaimed. "I just thought I was coming here for a dinner and to meet some of the other athletes."

After he won this prestigious award, Abbott garnered even more attention from the press and public. To him, it posed an unwanted distraction, both on and off the field. Throughout his first two and a half years of college, Abbott, a communications major, had been a solid B student. But now, swamped by demands for interviews and public appearances, Abbott fell behind in his classwork and his grades started to drop off. Fortunately, he noticed the danger signals in time and reapplied himself to his studies. Once Abbott took his spring semester final exams, his grades were back up to par.

Abbott also felt that the post–Sullivan Award hoopla had affected his performance on the mound. "I had a rocky season at Michigan," he claimed. "My concentration wasn't that good after the Sullivan Award." Still, it's hard to complain about a 9-3 record, a 3.32 ERA, eight complete games in 16 starts, 82 strikeouts and only 56 walks in 97⅔ innings, and back-to-back shutouts. Abbott also helped lead the Wolverines to a first-place regular-season finish and was named the Big Ten Player of the Year—not bad for a rocky junior year.

But would there be a senior year? As a college junior, Abbott once again was eligible for Major League Baseball's amateur draft, to be held on June 1. When he was a high school senior, he had been chosen by Toronto in the last round of the draft, but opted for college instead. This time, however, Abbott announced that he would turn pro if he were drafted.

There were no ifs about it. The influential publication *Baseball America* projected Abbott as a mid-second-round pick and rated him the top left-handed pitching prospect. As it turned out, the California Angels selected him high in the first round, making Abbott the eighth player chosen in the entire draft. "We decided he was the best left-hander in the draft," Angels scout George Bradley announced. "He's got the best fastball we've seen. He's the best all-around pitcher we've seen. And we felt he was far enough along that it won't take him as long to get to the majors as some of the other pitchers available."

California's director of scouting, Bob Fontaine, con-
curred. "He's actually more suited to the pro game than the
amateurs with the aluminum bats," Fontaine noted. "He's going
to break off a lot of these wood bats with that cut fastball."

As far as the Angels organization was concerned, Abbott's fielding was a non-issue. "We looked very closely at the
fielding aspect," Bradley disclosed. "We analyzed it and cross-
checked it. We had a lot of people see him and the consensus is
that he handles it very well. He can field bunts and defend his
position."

Opposing hitters long ago stopped trying to bunt against
Abbott once his barehanded plays had sent enough of them
back to the bench. As for those hot shots up the middle, "the
comebacker is a tough play if you've got two hands," he argued.
"You see major-league pitchers on the disabled list from a comebacker."

Possibly, Abbott thought, this play would pose less of a
problem in professional ball. "Those comebackers might be
even quicker off the aluminum bats we used in college," he continued. "That's one reason I'm looking forward to pitching in
spring training. But," he added cautiously, "with guys like José
Canseco and Mark McGwire swinging a wooden bat, a comebacker is pretty quick, too."

Of course, having been drafted by an American League
team, with the designated-hitter rule in effect, Abbott would
not have to worry about batting. "I guess they didn't know that I
hit .430 in high school with eight home runs," he said, in mock
disappointment. And in his three seasons at Michigan, Abbott
batted .667—that's two singles in three at bats. "But if they
threw a curveball," he admitted, "I couldn't touch it."

Before Abbott officially joined the Angels' organization, however, he decided to take care of one final bit of amateur
business. He was one of 40 college players invited to try out for

the United States Olympic baseball team. As expected, Abbott made the 20-member team and, once the school term ended, he headed for training camp in Millington, Tennessee, under the direction of Team USA's 1988 coach, Mark Marquess of Stanford.

On June 10, Team USA began a worldwide tour that would culminate in late September at the Summer Olympic Games in Seoul, South Korea. The exhausting three-and-a-half-month itinerary included seven games in various U.S. cities against the Cuban national team, a five-game series in Tulsa, Oklahoma, against the Korean team, a tour of Japan, visits to Hong Kong and India, and a trip to the biennial world amateur baseball championships in Italy.

"It was grueling," Abbott recalled the following summer. "We were in foreign countries, eating food we weren't used to. You couldn't find anything. Everything was awfully hard. But I think it helped mature me. . . . I can now appreciate what it's like to be 8,000 miles away with three weeks to go before you get back."

At the world championships, Team USA, as expected, faced Cuba in the gold-medal game. Abbott, the starting pitcher, took a 3-1 lead and a three-hit, eight-strikeout performance into the ninth inning, when Cuba's leadoff hitter reached first base on a close, controversial call. The next batter, Lourdes Gurriel, hit a two-run homer to tie the game, and Marquess decided to bring in Andy Benes to relieve Abbott. Cuba loaded the bases with a single, bunt single, sacrifice fly, and intentional walk, and scored the gold medal-winning run on a fly ball over the right fielder's head.

For Abbott, the highlight of the summer must have been the series in Japan against that country's national team. He was greatly impressed by the caliber of baseball played in Japan.

"The Japanese are smart players," Abbott remarked shortly before the Olympics. "They're so fundamentally sound, they never make a mistake. . . . They know how to go the other way, how to bunt. Their pitchers are always on the corners. And their fans are great."

For their part, the Japanese fans were even more taken with Abbott. His reputation had preceded him, and the people were fascinated with his story. "My picture was in the paper every day," Abbott recalled a year later, still incredulous. "There was a constant amount of attention.

"When we first practiced there, I fielded a bunt and cameras went off by the millions. Before I left a lady gave me a scrapbook and there was a huge layout, frame by frame, of me turning the glove over." In a little more than a week, Abbott became a national hero in Japan. Through nine and two-thirds innings of work, he allowed no runs, one hit, and struck out eight. The following spring, before Abbott ever threw a pitch in the majors, his picture appeared on the front cover of the Japanese edition of Street and Smith's 1989 preseason baseball guide.

Team USA ended its pre-Olympic tour and headed for Seoul with Abbott as the top starter on a strong pitching staff. He won seven games and lost one with a 2.59 ERA, striking out 63 batters and walking just 34 in 76⅓ innings. Abbott's lone defeat of the summer came in a 2-1 heartbreaker against Cuba. He was cruising along when, in the ninth inning, he hung a 95-mile-an-hour fastball out in the strike zone and the Cuban batter, Juan Castro, turned it around for a game-winning homer.

For the second consecutive Olympic Games, baseball was being played as a "demonstration sport." (It would become a full-fledged medal event in 1992.) The athletes on the top three teams would receive "commemorative" gold, silver, and bronze medals. Team USA arrived in Seoul as one of the favored teams, along with the defending Olympic champions, Japan, and the strong Canadian team. World champion Cuba was boycotting the games for political reasons.

Abbott immediately emerged as a favorite among the Korean press and public, receiving the same sort of attention and adulation that he had enjoyed in Japan. Photos of his arrival at Seoul's Kimpo Airport graced the local sports pages and his picture appeared on the cover of *Baseball Week*, the country's national baseball magazine.

The Olympic baseball tournament began on September 19, Abbott's 21st birthday, but Coach Marquess had no plans to use Abbott in that day's game against South Korea. The host team had few left-handed hitters and, the coach reasoned, it would be wiser to start right-hander Ben McDonald against them. The strategy worked, and Team USA won, 5-3. Two days later, another righty, Andy Benes, got the call for the second game, a 12-2 rout over Australia. Marquess was saving Abbott for the final first-round game against Canada, a team laced with lefty batters.

Between games, Abbott made the most of his Olympic experience and acted more like a wide-eyed tourist than a well-traveled athlete. "You go down to eat in the cafeteria and every day you see a [Matt] Biondi or a Steffi Graf," he marveled. "I had my picture taken with Gabriella Sabatini and *that* was real nice." Tennis star Pam Shriver wished him a happy birthday. Rubbing elbows with champion swimmers, tennis players, and the like, Abbott seemed to forget that he also was a world-class athlete. Otherwise, he wouldn't be there.

His camera was Abbott's constant companion. However, the camera is a product of a two-handed—and right-hand-ed—world, so Abbott had to adapt it to his special circumstance. The solution was simple: he held the camera crooked in his left arm, upside down, and worked the shutter with his left hand. "People see me do that," he laughed, "and they say, 'Hey, you gotta turn it around.' They don't realize the pictures come out the same."

Having won its first two games, Team USA was assured of a slot in the medal round. As a result, the Canada game served as a tune-up outing for Abbott, who was slated to start the gold-medal game regardless of the opponent. He pitched three scoreless innings against Canada, allowing four singles and striking out seven. Marquess wanted his left-hander ready, rested, and sharp for the finals, so he went to the bullpen earlier than usual. The United States ended up losing, 8-7, but the point was moot.

Three days later, McDonald pitched his second complete game of the Olympics as Team USA beat Puerto Rico, 7-2, in the semifinal game. The stage was now set for a September 28 rematch of the 1984 Olympic finals between the United States and Japan. In Los Angeles four years earlier, Japan had defeated the United States team to win the gold medal. This would be Abbott's last game as an amateur, and easily his biggest.

Japan jumped out to a 1-0 lead against Abbott in the second inning. Japan's starter, Takehiro Ishii, had thrown 100 pitches in the semifinal game two days earlier, and by the third inning, he began showing signs of strain. First baseman Tino Martinez blasted a 410-foot, two-run homer to straightaway center field, putting Team USA on top. They added another run in that inning, and one more in the next, on Martinez's RBI single, to give Abbott a 4-1 lead.

In the bottom of the sixth, Terushi Nakajimi hit a lead-off double and Takeshi Omori followed with a single. With runners on first and third and no outs, Abbott was in serious trouble. He struck out the following hitter, but walked the next two, forcing in a run. With the bases still loaded, pinch hitter Kenji Tomashino, swinging at Abbott's 2-0 pitch, hit a grounder that should have resulted in an inning-ending double play. Instead, only one out was made and another run crossed the plate.

With the score now 4-3, Marquess nearly brought in Andy Benes to relieve his faltering starter. "It was very close," Team USA's coach admitted later. "But I turned to one of my assistants and said, 'We gotta stay with him a little longer, because he's still got his good stuff.' "

Suddenly Abbott rediscovered his groove and started throwing strikes again. He got out of the sixth inning without any further damage and retired Japan three-up, three-down, in the seventh. In the top of the eighth, Martinez hit his second home run of the game, a 328-foot solo shot into the left-field corner, padding Team USA's lead to 5-3. As the scoreboard in Seoul's Chamsil Stadium flashed *Home Run,* the loudspeakers blared "Surfin' USA" by the Beach Boys.

Omori led off the bottom of the eighth with a single. The next batter, Hirofumi Ogawa, hit a tough one-hopper up the middle and right back at Abbott. He was thinking, "Double play," but the hard shot struck the side of his glove, which was balanced on the end of his right arm and bounced 10 feet away. Abbott pounced on the ball, shoveled it to Martinez at first, and fell face forward, as the out call was made. The following two hitters grounded out, second to first, and the potential rally was quashed before it started.

On to the bottom of the ninth, three outs to the gold medal. The Japanese batters were impatient and Abbott needed only four pitches to induce three straight ground balls to third baseman Robin Ventura. The two-time *Sporting News* College Player of the Year from Oklahoma State scooped up each one and threw in time to first. Abbott had retired 11 of the last 12 batters and pitched Team USA to an Olympic gold medal.

Tino Martinez, the hitting star of the game, stepped on first base for the final out and ran toward the mound to congratulate his pitcher. Abbott spread out his arms to receive his teammate, as the rest of the ecstatic gold-medal players stampeded to the center of the diamond. They knocked Abbott down and piled on top of him, nearly squashing him.

"I was right on the bottom," he laughed afterward, "with my face in the dirt, and my hand did get hurt." He actually had to check his throbbing wrist to make sure nothing was broken. Satisfied that his pitching hand was still in one piece, Abbott walked to the Japanese dugout for a sportsmanlike postgame handshake. Meanwhile, the revelry continued: his teammates ran a victory lap in the outfield, dumped a cooler of water over Marquess, and lobbed baseballs into the stands, delighting the cheering crowd with free souvenirs.

"It's a heck of a way to go out as an amateur," Abbott declared after the game, already anticipating the next stage in his baseball career. "I hope it carries over. I know pro is a whole new ballgame, but I think I'm ready for that challenge. It's time for something new."

In late August, barely a month before the Olympics, the California Angels signed Abbott to a contract with their Midland, Texas, double-A farm club and paid him a reported $207,500 bonus. On the day he won the gold-medal game, Abbott insisted that going to college was "the best decision I've ever made," and he undoubtedly meant it. Nevertheless, the following February, he left the University of Michigan, put his studies on hold, and headed for his first professional training camp.

"I always thought I would play pro ball," Abbott declared when the Angels drafted him. "I didn't think about any-thing holding me back. . . . I figured I'd play until someone took my spikes away and told me I wasn't good enough anymore." At last, Abbott's dream was within his reach, and he was not about to make it wait for anything. He could finish college anytime, but this was something he had to do, and *now*.

4

∼○ Rookie

When the California Angels opened their 1989 training camp in Mesa, Arizona, Jim Abbott was not the only newcomer to the team. The Angels also had a new manager, former big-league third baseman Doug Rader. As a player, Rader spent 11 years in the majors, nine of them with the Houston Astros, and was known for a scrappy, pugnacious manner that earned him the nickname the "Red Rooster."

This would be Rader's second stint at the helm of a big-league club. In 1983, saddled with a weak franchise and unsupportive ownership, Rader somehow pulled the Texas Rangers to a surprising third-place finish. However, the team returned to its true level in 1984 and sank to last place. When Rader's Rangers started the 1985 season with just nine wins in their first 34 games, the Red Rooster got the ax. Now he was back, preparing for another bittersweet taste of life as a major-league manager.

Ever since the Angels entered the American League in 1961, they have been a study in futility and frustration. With the advent of free agency in the late 1970s, owner Gene Autry, the singing cowboy of B-movie fame, began using his vast wealth to stock his team with high-priced, big-name stars. Many times the Angels looked like potential champions—they even made it to the playoffs three times (1979, 1982, and 1986)—but they always managed to disappoint their long-suffering fans. And so, Rader's task was simple: win it all as soon as possible. Of course, that's the job of every big-league manager.

But as spring training approached, the Angels' new manager was overshadowed by an even bigger story. Jim Abbott, the one-handed college phenom and first-round draft pick, was about to experience his first major-league training camp. Reporters and fans alike wondered whether Abbott could make the club straight out of college, without spending time in the minors.

That doesn't happen often, and when it does, you're usually talking about one of the game's all-time greats, like Walter Johnson, Mel Ott, Bob Feller, Ernie Banks (who did play one year in the old Negro leagues), or Al Kaline. From 1965, the first year of the amateur draft, to 1988, only 15 players made their professional debut in the majors with no prior minor-league experience. One is a future Hall of Famer, Dave Winfield. A small number of them, like Burt Hooton and Bob Horner, enjoyed solid big-league careers.

But just as often, these highly touted phenoms toiled through undistinguished and forgettable spells, and pitchers tend to be especially prone to this fate. Few remember Steve Dunning—23 wins and 41 losses over seven seasons—or David Clyde—an 18-33 record in five years. Others seemed to vanish from the scene as quickly as they appeared, like Mike Adamson (0-4 with a 7.46 ERA in three seasons) and Eddie Bane (7-13 in three years).

So it was unlikely that Jim Abbott would jump right from college to the majors. Even if he did, his chances for a successful rookie season were slim. The combined first-year record of the eight pitchers who, between 1965 and 1988, made their professional debuts in the major leagues is a dismal 21-44. Only one of them, Hooton, posted a winning record as a rookie: two wins, no losses.

Rader, who had not yet seen Abbott pitch in person, was well aware of these long odds and emphasized that he had no plans to rush the 21-year-old pitcher into the majors. "I think it would be a little unfair," he told the *Los Angeles Times* in late January, "for anybody to think that Jim Abbott will make the club in spring training."

Of course, Rader was aware of the scouting reports, and he felt that a player with Abbott's potential should progress swiftly through the minors. "Then again," the manager added, "I don't think anybody in the entire Angels organization would be reluctant to say that they wouldn't be surprised to see Jim Abbott pitching with the team before the year is out."

Abbott arrived at the Angels' camp in mid-February, one of only eight nonroster players invited to train with the major leaguers. He was assigned uniform number 60. Teams normally give the higher numbers to the rookies who are not likely to be with the club at the end of spring. Abbott was slated to start the regular season with California's double-A farm team in Midland, Texas.

The organization felt that Abbott needed to develop a more consistent curveball to go with his hard-breaking slider and 94-mile-an-hour fastball, and you don't do that in big-league games against big-league hitters. In addition, California's starting rotation was set. Barring injury, there was no place for Abbott on the Angels' 24-man major-league roster.

But that didn't reduce the hoopla and hype surrounding Abbott's appearance in camp. Mike Penner of the *Los Angeles Times* observed cynically—or realistically, depending on one's perspective—that his presence "has almost as much to do with public relations value as potential. He's a good story now," Penner noted, "but probably doesn't contend for an Angel roster spot until later," which is what Rader had said in January.

For his part, Abbott was thrilled to be working out with the big guys. The first hitter he pitched against in batting practice was Lance Parrish, the former Detroit Tigers catcher whom Abbott used to watch at Tiger Stadium. And there he was, 60 feet, six inches, away, "the first guy I ever faced with a wooden bat," said Abbott, barely concealing his awe.

After his turn at bat, Parrish donned his catcher's armor and moved behind the plate, as even more childhood memories flooded Abbott's mind. How many times, on television or at the ballpark, had he seen Parrish's orange-rimmed catcher's mitt aimed at Jack Morris, Dan Petry, or Frank Tanana? Now, at his first big-league training camp, he's looking straight into that familiar target himself. "There it is," Abbott marveled, "staring right at you."

Afterward, the veteran catcher offered his assessment of the youngster. "He probably has as strong an arm as any left-hander I've ever caught," Parrish observed. "His motion is so fluid, the ball just kind of explodes." He compared Abbott's fastball to that of Ron Guidry, the New York Yankees' star left-hander of the 1970s and 1980s. Bullpen coach Joe Coleman had a comparison of his own, likening Abbott's smooth windup and delivery to that of Hall of Famer Steve Carlton.

Abbott made his much anticipated Angels debut on

March 3, in a B squad game against the San Diego Padres. The B squad is the spring-training equivalent of junior varsity, a collection of hopeful young walk-ons aching for a shot, nearly washed-up veterans trying to prolong their careers, and a few real prospects, like Abbott. In other words, the B squad is the domain of rookies, scrubs, has-beens, and never-will-bes. Its early spring-training games are of interest to no one, other than the desperate players' friends and family—unless, of course, Jim Abbott is scheduled to pitch.

Suddenly, the Angels' B squad became the stuff of headlines. To accommodate the extraordinary public and media presence, the game had to be moved from the side practice field to the main stadium in the Padres' Yuma, Arizona, training complex. A press conference was scheduled to be held 45 minutes after Abbott's last pitch—in the early spring, pitchers normally work no longer than three innings—even though the game would not yet be over.

Abbott was the second Angel pitcher slated to work that day. Windy conditions threatened to make pitching difficult, and the Angels' starter struggled, allowing four hits and three walks in three innings. But the much heralded rookie came in and blew away the Padres' hitters. Abbott struck out his first two batters on just seven pitches and worked the third hitter to an 0-2 count, before he reached base on an error. Unfazed, Abbott retired the next four batters. In three innings, he struck out four and gave up two hits, no walks, and no runs.

"Everybody's in the dugout going, 'Yeah, check this guy out,'" observed Carmelo Martinez, one of Abbott's strikeout victims, "and for my first at bat it was hard to concentrate. But then you realize that the ball comes from the same place and goes to the same place. If you're looking at just his arm, he's got you."

At last, Rader had seen Abbott pitch in person, and he

was ecstatic. "How about that first batter?" the manager asked the reporters. "Wham, wham, see you later. The level of his maturity and his composure and his stability, I can't tell you how wonderful it is. All the accolades he's received are richly deserved."

At the press conference, Abbott fielded the reporters' questions with poise and, as usual, seemed bemused by all the attention. "I've been doing this since I was five years old," he told them. "Now it's just as natural as tying my shoes." It was either an unwitting joke or a subtle dig. After all, to a two-handed sports writer, tying your shoes with one hand is as incredible a feat as pitching a baseball that way.

Four days later, Abbott appeared in his first A squad game, pitching two innings against the Oakland Athletics in Phoenix. He yielded one hit and three walks and allowed a run to score when he bobbled a comeback grounder that would have been an inning-ending double play. But Abbott also struck out two batters, including a two-out whiff of José Canseco, the 1988 American League Most Valuable Player, with runners on second and third.

"He was trying to overthrow [to] the first couple batters he faced," Lance Parrish explained. "His second inning was much better. I've been impressed with him ever since he's been here. . . . [This outing] wasn't a fair viewing. It was his first time. I've caught him in the batting cage a few times and he's almost torn the glove off my hand. He throws as hard as anyone in camp."

On balance, it was a decent early-spring performance. Still, the Angels front office insisted that Abbott would start the year in double-A. "Those were our initial plans," said Rader, cautiously affirming the official line. "But by no means are they inflexible," he added. Clearly the new manager, at least, was keeping all his options open.

"If you're to be perfectly objective about it," Rader reasoned, "then he's certainly one of the 10 best pitchers in our organization. And if he's one of the 10 best we have, how can we not have him on our pitching staff?"

Even though little had changed—Abbott was still a two-pitch pitcher and the status of the veteran starters remained the overriding factor—the very next day, Rader seemed to inch a bit closer to having Abbott open the season with the big club. "I think Abbie is the kind of guy who, emotionally and physically, could probably play in the big leagues right now," he asserted. Was Rader trying to convince his bosses in the Angel front office or himself? Maybe both.

In his next outing, against the Milwaukee Brewers, Abbott threw three strong innings, retiring the first six batters he faced. After the game, Rader disclosed that he would keep Abbott with the major-league club until the final roster cut, when the Angels moved to Palm Springs, California, for the last two weeks of spring training.

Parrish felt that his pitcher seemed more relaxed and confident on the mound than in his last appearance, and Abbott agreed. "The other day against Oakland," he noted, "I went out there and hurried too much. [Bullpen coach] Joe Coleman told me to slow down and take my time today, and the advice really paid off." Not only a strong prospect, Abbott was proving to be an apt pupil and a quick learner.

"If this keeps up much longer," wrote Mike Penner, "they're going to run out of reasons for keeping Abbott off the Angels' 24-man roster." Cooperative and polite with the press, Abbott had most of the local sports writers supporting his cause, and they could be a formidable ally.

Penner asked Abbott whether he thought he had a chance to make the club. The rookie, as always, answered cautiously and diplomatically. Yet, an appealing big-league cockiness peeked through his reply. "I don't think anybody comes to camp thinking, 'I have no chance,' " Abbott responded. "Everybody hopes to make it.

"I'm being realistic about it," he went on. "So far in spring training, I think I've improved to where this will serve as a good springboard into the season, wherever I end up." With the help of his boosters in the press, Abbott was putting the Angels' management on notice. "I've done everything I could to show you that I belong here, and that I should stay here," was what he seemed to be telling them, in his own careful and gentle way.

Finally, fate intervened. Veteran right-hander Dan Petry had suffered a rotator cuff strain in his pitching shoulder that was slow to heal. He fell behind the rest of the starting rotation in preparing for the season, and when he did pitch he was erratic. Rader announced that he was concerned about Petry's status. Somewhere in the back of the manager's mind he must have sensed that this might be his excuse to keep Abbott around beyond Opening Day.

As the last days of March passed, the Angels began announcing their final roster moves. The biggest news, however, was what the team didn't do: it didn't send Abbott down to its double-A farm team in Midland, Texas (or its triple-A club in Edmonton, Canada, for that matter). Still, no one would say what was becoming more and more obvious, that he now was virtually assured of a spot on the Opening Day roster, and maybe even the starting rotation.

Rader was both cagey and revealing. "Jim deserves to be in this position," he observed. "It's very encouraging for him to be coming down to competing for the final spot and a starting job." He also offered an unsolicited, and convincing, defense of Abbott's rather high 5.54 spring ERA. "There's been only two balls hit hard off him," the manager argued. "The last time he pitched he gave up four broken-bat hits." As for the wounded Petry, Rader indicated that, "at this point, he's not quite ready to be a starter."

On March 29, Abbott got his first start of the spring. He pitched just four innings against the Padres, giving up two runs on six hits in a losing cause. Nevertheless, he walked only one batter and fanned three, including Tony Gwynn, one of the game's best hitters and hardest men to strike out.

After the game, Rader announced that, despite this less-than-spectacular outing, Abbott would be the Angels' number-five starter. His regular-season debut was slated for April 8 at Anaheim Stadium against the Seattle Mariners. Dan Petry would start the season in long relief, the dumping ground for pitchers who either can no longer pitch or never could.

As a matter of fact, Abbott's performance that day was immaterial. Rader revealed that he knew what he was going to do even before the game. And judging from his statements to the press, the Angels manager probably made up his mind about Abbott days, if not weeks, earlier.

For example, Rader, as quoted in the previous week's issue of the *Sporting News*, seemed to be paving the way for the big decision. "Historically, there's been a tendency not to take the best 10 arms, which I think is a mistake," the manager asserted. "If he [Abbott] is one of them, he should stay."

At first, Rader thought it might be best to let Abbott get his feet wet by working in relief. That way, he figured, the rookie might be under less pressure and have fewer problems with the press. "But then I realized that was silly," he admitted. "Jim was able to handle 25-man press conferences when we were training in Mesa, Arizona."

And so, after nearly two months of evaluating Abbott's

skills and considering his options, Rader reached an inevitable conclusion. "I've slowly been brought around to the idea," the manager announced, "that unless he starts, his ability won't be best served."

Rader also revealed that Angels pitching coach Marcel Lachemann helped influence his decision. "Abbott has three things going for him," Rader declared, "maturity, tremendous talent, and Marcel Lachemann." Lachemann was, from the first, Abbott's biggest supporter in the Angels organization. In the future, when the going would get tough and Abbott would face some harsh and unfair criticism, Lachemann would remain steadfast in Abbott's corner.

Like every other milestone in his young career, Abbott's major-league debut was part baseball game, part circus. Reporters, photographers, and camera operators representing newspapers, magazines, and television networks throughout America flooded Anaheim Stadium to cover the big event. Four television crews came all the way from Japan to bring the story back to their baseball-mad country.

As Abbott, now wearing number 25, a big-leaguer's number, took the mound for the top of the first, he received a huge ovation from the 46,847 fans in attendance. They were expecting something memorable, even historic, forgetting that what they had come to see was merely the first major-league start by an untested rookie pitcher. And, thanks to a combination of nerves, an ill-timed defensive lapse, and plain old bad luck, that is exactly what they got.

In the top of the first, a pair of back-to-back singles and a wild pitch suddenly gave the Mariners runners on second and third with no outs. Both runners scored on consecutive groundouts to second, before Abbott ended the inning with a third grounder. With one big-league inning under his belt, Abbott already was down 2-0.

"There was definitely some nervousness there," he said later. "Maybe I wasn't as clearly focused as I should have been." But Abbott quickly settled down, retiring the Mariners in order in the second inning. In the third, he worked his way out of a one-out, bases-loaded jam by getting the batter to ground into an inning-ending double play. The fourth inning was like the second—three up, three down.

Then, with one out in the fifth, the wheels, as they say, came off the cart. Omar Vizquel singled to left. Harold Reynolds hit a high bouncer to Angel second baseman Mark McLemore that might have resulted in a double play. However, McLemore took his eye off the ball and botched the play. Instead of being out of the inning, Abbott now had runners on second and third. "I thought the pitch I made to Reynolds was the best pitch I made all night," Abbott lamented. "But sometimes things don't work out."

An intentional walk to Henry Cotto loaded the bases, bringing up Alvin Davis. Quickly Abbott put him in a no-ball, two-strike hole, but Davis looped the next pitch into short right field for a broken-bat single, driving in two runs. "I did what I wanted to Davis," Abbott explained. "I got a fastball up and in, but he just fought it off. Those kinds of plays are the most frustrating, the toughest to live with." He threw two good pitches, but because of an error and a solid piece of defensive hitting, two runs had crossed the plate, Mariners stood on first and third, and Abbott still had just one out.

Darnell Coles forced Davis at second, driving in Cotto from third. Jeffrey Leonard's two-out, line-drive single to left scored Coles, and that was all for Abbott. As he handed the ball to Rader and walked off to the mound, on the way to his first major-league loss, the crowd stood and cheered with appreciation. Abbott was grateful but, he shrugged, "That was one ovation I wish I hadn't gotten."

Rader tried to put a positive spin on his rookie's performance. "Under the conditions, I thought he pitched outstanding. Had it not been for a misplayed ball and a bloop hit, it would have been a different ballgame." And it was true that Abbott got little help from his teammates, who managed only six hits against Seattle's ace left-hander Mark Langston in the 7-0 defeat.

Still, Abbott knew that he was anything but outstanding that night, and the numbers showed it. In four and two-thirds innings Abbott gave up six runs (three of them earned) on six hits, three walks (one intentional), and a wild pitch. He struck out no one, had two strikes on only five of the 24 hitters he faced, and only twice did a batter swing at and miss one of his pitches. "I don't think I threw too well," he admitted. "I felt I sometimes battled OK and made some pitches I'm proud of, but overall I didn't do as much as I'm capable of."

Yet, on the positive side, 13 of 24 Mariners batters hit the ball on the ground—a sign that Abbott was making good pitches, keeping the ball down—and he gave up no extra-base hits. Harold Reynolds, the beneficiary of McLemore's error, was impressed. "I was surprised at how hard he threw," the Seattle second baseman told reporters. "Nobody got any great swings against him and nobody was teeing off on him. I think the man is going to be a big-league pitcher for a long, long time."

In his next start, at home against the Oakland Athletics five days later, Abbott pitched in and out of jams, was victimized by more poor fielding and again received no run support. Through five innings he was behind just 1-0 and, with a little luck, it appeared that he might notch his first career victory.

Terry Steinbach, leading off the Oakland half of the sixth inning, hit a deep, but catchable, fly to right field. Angels right fielder Claudell Washington chased it, ran into the wall, and allowed the ball to hit the fence, below his glove, giving Steinbach what was scored as a double. The next hitter, Carney Lansford, hit a bouncer to second base that caromed off Mark McLemore's leg for an error.

With runners on first and third, Dave Parker grounded a potential double-play ball to McLemore, who wrestled with it and wound up with only a force at second, as Steinbach scored. Two more runs came in on a two-out double by Mike Gallego. Abbott left the game after the inning having pitched well, but down 4-0. The California offense was held to just four hits by Oakland starter Mike Moore and reliever Dennis Eckersley, and Abbott was saddled with a tough 5-0 loss.

Abbott missed his next scheduled start in Chicago when the game was postponed because of cold weather and the threat of snow. Eleven days passed before he took the mound again, in Anaheim against the Baltimore Orioles on April 25. The two losses and the unexpected period of inactivity had begun to bother him. "I wasn't contributing," Abbott said with concern, "and sometimes you feel like you don't belong."

All he really needed was a victory, and at last it came. It was not the most artistic of performances. Abbott had trouble throwing strikes and holding runners. In six innings he gave up two runs on four hits, walking three and striking out just one, and allowing a wild pitch and three stolen bases. But he left the game leading, 3-2. For a change, the Angels batters, shut out in Abbott's first two starts, had scored some runs for him.

Anticipation turned into anxiety, and nearly disappointment, when the Orioles loaded the bases with two out in the eighth inning. As Abbott watched nervously on the clubhouse television, Angels reliever Bryan Harvey fell into a three-ball, one-strike hole against pinch hitter Jim Traber. But Harvey hung in and struck Traber out to end the threat.

"I jumped up and down a little," Abbott revealed. "I guess it's a good thing I wasn't in the dugout. I've been taking a lot of flak for acting like a rookie." But the Angels bench was just as nervous and just as excited when the inning was over. "If the team doctor hadn't been sitting in my lap," Rader joked, "I don't think I could've gotten through the eighth." Harvey retired the Orioles one-two-three in the ninth, and Abbott got his win.

Since the start of the season, Rader had been second-guessed on the local radio call-in sports shows for having "rushed" Abbott to the majors. After the first two losses, he may have harbored doubts of his own, although he never expressed them. But now, he had proven that the armchair managers and get-a-life windbags were wrong. "Vindication is not the right word for how I feel," Rader announced. "Relief is." Abbott also was relieved. "Now I feel more and more like a member of the Angels," he said, "like I belong."

But he needn't have worried. Abbott's teammates warmed to the outgoing, enthusiastic rookie, and in no time he became one of the guys. Perhaps the most genuine expression of how the Angels veterans felt about Abbott occurred after his May 17 complete-game victory over the Boston Red Sox and their then-two-time Cy Young Award winner, Roger Clemens. Abbott yielded just four hits and two walks, striking out four, to shut out the Red Sox, 5-0. In honor of his sterling performance, Abbott's teammates set down a carpet of white towels leading to his locker, the baseball equivalent of the "red carpet treatment." He was now an Angels VIP—"Very Important Pitcher."

The feeling that you belong in the big leagues is something each rookie struggles to achieve, and it rises and falls with his performance. The normally confident and self-assured Jim Abbott, an athlete who had conquered all previous obstacles, began experiencing occasional, nagging self-doubts. "Some days it seems like I have the best job in the world," he reflected. "Living in California down by the beach, playing baseball in the major leagues. Other days I really feel the insecurity of it."

Former big-league pitcher and pitching coach Johnny Sain had a theory about winning. "He used to say," explained author, ex-major leaguer, and Sain protegé Jim Bouton, "a pitcher had a special kind of feeling after he did really well in a ballgame. John called it the cool of the evening, when you could sit and relax and not worry about being in there for three or four more days; the job [was] done, a good job, and now it was up to somebody else to go out there the next day and do the slogging."

Abbott experienced this sensation after his first victory, and he savored it. "I had the most incredible euphoria," he recalled. "I just wanted to hold on to it. I'd say there's nothing better than pitching a game and doing well. Nothing."

On the other hand, when a pitcher has been shelled, the old insecurity returns and time passes slowly until his next start. A hitter can have a bad game and return to the action the next day, ready to take on the world. But "if a pitcher doesn't do well," Bouton observed, "he has three or four days to contemplate his sins."

Abbott knew that feeling all too well. "When you've pitched and done poorly," he told *Life* magazine early in his rookie season, "it's a lonely, hollow feeling, like you let the whole world down. . . . You've got to suffer through that for five days."

The trick is to keep it all in perspective. You can't let the highs get you too up, or the lows get you too down. *Los Angeles Times* sports writer Scott Ostler observed how Abbott "marvels at the vets like [Bert] Blyleven, who shake off a loss as easily as they nonchalant a shutout." Of course, that kind of maturity is rare in a 21-year-old rookie and comes only with time and experience. Still, you had better develop it if you want to last a while in the big leagues.

On June 17, a man stopped by the visitors' clubhouse at Tiger Stadium in Detroit. The Angels were in town, and he was hoping to visit with Jim Abbott. Despite his obvious credentials, a baseball cap that proudly declared, "Abbott's Grandpa," he could not convince the guard to let him in. But it was true. Abbott's grandfather, along with 57 other relatives and friends, had come from nearby Flint, courtesy of the Angels' pass list, to cheer for Abbott as he took the mound for the first time against the team he once rooted for, the Detroit Tigers.

"This was certainly a longtime dream for me," he said after the game. "I grew up here and this is my idea of what major-league baseball is all about. But after the first couple of innings, I was quickly reminded it's a game—and you better concentrate on pitching your game."

He started out a bit rocky. Abbott gave up a first-inning home run to Tracy Jones, a .186 hitter, and a home run in the second to Gary Ward, a New York Yankees castoff whom the Tigers had acquired on waivers the previous month. But he eventually settled down and allowed just five singles, one walk, and one more run over the next five innings. He left the game after the seventh, and the Angels held on to win, 6-3, Abbott's sixth victory in ten decisions.

Having Lance Parrish, a veteran catcher and a former Tiger, handling his pitches was a big plus for Abbott. "I just tried to have him go at it like any other day," Parrish explained, "and not let the outside influences get in his way. I didn't want him to get too excited and overthrow the ball."

Aside from those two homers to a couple of scrubs, Rader felt that Abbott pitched an otherwise flawless game, consistently keeping the ball down in the strike zone, the spot where he is most effective. "He got just two balls up," the manager noted. "A high change-up to Jones, a high fastball to Ward. Those were the only two bad pitches he threw."

The last time a road trip had taken the Angels through Detroit, a rainout in Toronto forced Rader to shift his pitching rotation, and Abbott was disappointed when he missed a scheduled start before the hometown fans. Now that he had gotten his chance and made the most of it, he had to confess that he was glad it was over. "I don't think I want to throw here again," he said in the locker room, with a combination of achievement and relief.

Abbott was maturing with every start, developing as a pitcher and a major leaguer each time he took the mound. "His capacity to learn and his resiliency after making mistakes are the reasons he's here," Rader observed near midseason, "other than being blessed with a great left arm." Of course, Abbott was prone to the occasional rookie mistake, and one time in particular, he needed all the resiliency he could muster to recover from it.

Abbott's bonehead play occurred in an early-July game against the Minnesota Twins in Anaheim. With two out in the third inning, a 0-0 score, and Al Newman on first base, Twins batter Greg Gagne hit a grounder to first. Wally Joyner fielded the ball and Abbott hustled over to cover the bag and receive the throw. It was a close play, and first-base umpire Tim Tschida called Gagne safe. Abbott argued the call, forgetting all about Newman, who was able to sprint to third while Abbott mindlessly held onto the ball.

Abbott returned to the mound, visibly upset with this lapse in concentration. Pitching coach Marcel Lachemann and catcher Lance Parrish came out to try and calm him down.

Standing in the batter's box was Kirby Puckett, the American League's leading hitter, so this was no time to lose his composure. Instead, Abbott turned his anger outward. He began firing pitches at the plate and never let up until a high, hard, mid-90s fastball whizzed past Puckett for strike three, ending the jam.

"He was as upset as I've ever seen him for letting the guy get to third," Parrish told reporters with amusement and admiration. "And if there's any guy you can stand to get a little fired up for, it's Kirby."

Abbott went on to win the game, his eighth of the year, yielding only one run in six and one-third innings' work. Every one of his 19 outs was recorded on either a strikeout—and he had seven of those—or a groundball, and he allowed just one walk. Still, Abbott was not entirely satisfied with the strong outing.

"I gave up too many hits [nine], but they were all singles," he observed, "and not too damaging. Until I get a good third pitch, the good hitters are going to be able to fight off fastballs and hard sliders and get some hits."

There were other areas to work on as well. Left-handed pitchers are supposed to be hard to run on, but early in the season, opposing base runners were stealing on Abbott every chance they could get. In one early-May game against the Toronto Blue Jays, for example, Abbott was stolen on three times, including once by the slow-running catcher-DH Bob Brenly, who had swiped only one base in all of 1988. By the end of the season, Abbott had been stolen on 29 times in 181⅓ innings, an average of 1.44 stolen bases per every nine innings, which made him the second-easiest pitcher to steal on in the American League.

Abbott's delivery, with its high leg kick, was easy to read, and baserunners could tell whether he would be throwing home or over to first. Clearly Abbott needed to learn how to use a slide step with runners on base. By sliding his front leg toward home plate, instead of raising it in the air, as he delivered the pitch, he could hold runners closer to first base and reduce the number of stolen bases.

The old questions about Abbott's ability to field his position also began to pop up, and not without reason. As the season progressed, it became clear that Abbott was missing a lot of plays that he should have made. "Actually I'm kinda' disgusted with myself," he revealed in August. "Some of those balls that have been hit past me, I used to field with nonchalance. . . . I don't know if I'm concentrating too much on pitching, but I'm trying to keep it from becoming a big thing."

Certainly Abbott's mechanics were sound, and his form—the glove-hand switch notwithstanding—was almost textbook. Far too many pitchers either fall awkwardly off the mound or leave their glove hands behind their backs after they deliver the pitch. At the end of his follow-through, Abbott faces the hitter squarely, his glove out in front of him, ready to make the play on a batted ball through the middle. And so it seemed likely that, in time, his fielding problems would work themselves out.

In early July, Abbott set an obscure record, the kind of "milestone" that could have been noticed only in this statistics-obsessed age. His seventh win of the season set the mark for "most victories in his first major-league season by a pitcher who never pitched in the minor leagues since the inauguration of the amateur draft" (1965). Abbott laughed when informed of his feat. "Now there's one record I really haven't paid any attention to," he said with amusement.

More important than this oddball record was the fact that Abbott was one of the best rookie pitchers in baseball that year. He won a total of 12 games and made a valuable contribution to a vastly improved Angels team that for much of the season was in the division race and briefly occupied first place. The Los Angeles–Anaheim chapter of the Baseball Writers Association of America named him the Angels' Rookie of the Year and Most Inspirational Player for 1989.

California ended the season in third place, eight games behind the eventual world champion Oakland Athletics. Still, the Angels' 91-71 record was a 16-game improvement over its 1988 finish and, like Abbott's performance, a positive omen for 1990.

As far as pitching coach Marcel Lachemann was concerned, Abbott had demonstrated that he belonged in the majors and would be there to stay. "All the questions about him have pretty much been put aside," Lachemann maintained. "Some people worried that he couldn't field bunts. But he's been doing that all his life, and he's good on them. They worried that he'd get killed on a ball through the middle. . . . But a lot of pitchers have that problem.

"They said he couldn't hold runners on," the coach continued. "He had trouble early on, but he's learned a slide step and he's getting better all the time. Most important, he's proved he has quality major-league stuff—a great breaking ball, pitches inside to right-handers—and he seems to throw his best pitches when he's in jams."

Of course there was room for improvement. Abbott's strikeout-to-walk ratio was 1.55, slightly below the league average of 1.69 and rather low compared with other starting pitchers around the league and even on his own team. Angels ace Bert Blyleven, who posted an excellent 17-5 won-loss record that season, had a terrific strikeout-walk ratio, 2.98. Teammates Chuck Finley (16-9) and Kirk McCaskill (15-10) had figures of 1.90 and 1.81, respectively.

Other top ratios that season were achieved by Oak-land's Dave Stewart (21-9, 2.25 strikeouts to walks), Boston's Roger Clemens (17-11, 2.47), Nolan Ryan of Texas (16-10, 3.07), and the Cy Young Award winner, Kansas City's Bret Saberhagen (23-6, with an astounding 4.49 figure). But a high strikeout-to-walk ratio, though desirable, does not guarantee success. Abbott's Angels teammate Mike Witt logged 2.56 strikeouts for every walk, yet his 1989 record was a dismal 9-15, while Toronto's Dave Stieb finished a strong 17-8 with only a 1.33 ratio.

Likewise, Abbott allowed an average of 13.1 base run-ners (i.e., walks plus hits) per every nine innings pitched, an-other mark that needed improving. For comparison, Blyleven allowed 10.05 runners per nine innings, Ryan allowed 9.7, and Saberhagen led all of baseball with an 8.7 average. The more men a pitcher puts on base, the more runs he may allow, and the more games he is likely to lose. This was borne out by Abbott's 1989 record: 12 losses to go with his 12 wins and a rather high 3.92 earned run average. With the addition of *unearned* runs that were charged to him, Abbott actually yielded an average of 4.72 runs per nine innings.

But you can analyze the numbers all you want. The bot-tom line is that Jim Abbott came straight out of college and into the major leagues, performed effectively as a rookie, helped his team improve, and held the promise of even better things to come. Very few rookies in the entire history of the game have done that.

5

∿ο **A Reluctant Role Model**

When catcher Rick Turner learned that he would be rooming with Jim Abbott at the Angels' 1989 spring training camp, he thought he might have to help his fellow rookie with some everyday tasks. He soon discovered otherwise. "You don't have to ask him what he can't do," Turner declared. "Just sit back and watch what he *can* do."

That's all Abbott ever wanted. Still there was no escaping that this rookie was different. The attention he received was astounding and, at times, more than a little embarrassing.

"He is the Rookie of Spring," wrote Scott Ostler of the *Los Angeles Times,* "an unofficial title the world bestows on one unsuspecting kid. The title is both an honor and a potential curse, and the honoree receives, free of charge, a small army of reporters and photographers to follow him around . . . with relentless zeal."

Of course, in Abbott's case there was an added feature. He was a good player, but an even better headline: JIM ABBOTT, ONE-HANDED ROOKIE PITCHER. It seemed like every newspaper, magazine, and television station in the country, and a surprising number from abroad, had sent reporters and camera people to Mesa, Arizona, to record and rehash Abbott's story. Marcel Lachemann wondered whether, when all this attention finally subsided, Abbott would be able to pitch without the constant click, click, click of cameras.

Both *Sports Illustrated* and the *New York Times* profiled Abbott twice that season. *Time, Newsweek,* and the *Sporting News* ran flattering features on him. *Life* spent three-and-a-half hours on the beach with him for a photo shoot. He was interviewed on ESPN, CNN, and countless television and radio programs throughout the United States. No rookie ever received that kind of coverage.

Even before he pitched his first B squad game, Abbott received, and turned down, three book offers and a deal for a television movie about his life story. *Baseball America* ranked his major-league debut, in terms of its historical significance, behind only Jackie Robinson's breaking of the color barrier in 1947. Then there were those four Japanese television crews that arrived to chronicle his first start.

And the mail—by early May, Abbott had received literally thousands of fan letters. During road trips, the Angels publicity staff would collect Abbott's mail in a shopping cart and wheel it to him when he returned to Anaheim. "Jim has received more attention than any Angel I can remember," Angels public-relations director Tim Mead observed, "more than Wally Joyner when he was a rookie, more than Reggie Jackson, more than Rod Carew."

Even other players were awed by Abbott. On his first day in the majors, the clubhouse boy at Anaheim Stadium handed Abbott a telegram: "Congratulations. Looking forward to seeing you pitch this year. [signed] Nolan Ryan." Abbott was first stunned, then wary. Ballplayers are notorious practical jokers and he suspected the team's resident comedian, Bert Blyleven, of pulling his leg. But the message was real, and Abbott's teammates passed the telegram around the clubhouse with proper reverence.

Later that season, Abbott was visited in the Angels clubhouse by Hall of Famer Warren Spahn, one of the greatest left-handed pitchers of all time. "You're my hero," the 363-game winner told the rookie. Abbott simply didn't know what to say. "I think I need a few more wins to catch up to him," he remarked afterward, still in shock.

Two days later, the Angels hosted the Equitable Old-Timer's Game, reuniting many former baseball greats. Boston Red Sox Hall of Famer Bobby Doerr brought a baseball for Abbott to sign. Another all-time star, Ernie Banks, wanted his picture taken with him. "This is incredible," said the awestruck rookie.

To his credit, Abbott recognized that the interviews and the fan mail were the price of being a professional athlete. "I think of something [former major-league pitcher] Don Sutton said when I was with him this winter at a clinic," Abbott told the *Sporting News* that spring. "Someone asked him if he ever got tired of giving autographs. He told them, 'It's reasonable rent for the space you get to occupy.' I've tried to keep this in mind."

And so, he tried to enjoy it. "All the attention has been encouraging," Abbott maintained. "The best part about it is that it has been supportive. As long as it doesn't interfere with my job, I don't mind."

However, by the second week of spring training, Abbott

During 1945, with many able-bodied athletes serving in World War II (and blacks still barred from organized baseball), Gray played outfield for the St. Louis Browns. Groping for analogies, reporters continually asked Abbott, "Was Pete Gray your role model when you were growing up?"

In fact, the comparison between Gray and Abbott was no more than superficial. Hoping to boost their sagging wartime attendance, the Browns tried to manufacture Gray into a fan favorite, announcing his name last in the pregame player introductions. But on the field, Gray hit a mere .218 in 234 at bats and was out of the majors by the next season, once the soldier-ballplayers returned to civilian life.

Despite what a few cynics may have thought at first, Abbott's presence on the Angels' roster was no "publicity stunt," and he quickly proved it. Just ask the Red Sox batters after the rookie outdueled Roger Clemens and shut them out whether Abbott was a legitimate major-league pitcher. If Abbott were there only to sell tickets, his roommate Rick Turner argued, "we'd also have a 50-year-old pitcher, a 17-year-old, and a guy three feet tall on the team."

And in the opinion of someone who knew them both, Gray and Abbott were miles apart in terms of how they coped with their disabilities. Preston Gomez, a former big-league manager who was working in the Angels' front office, had played with Gray in the minors after the war. "Pete Gray lost his arm in a childhood accident," Gomez recalled. "He thought everybody was against him. Jim Abbott was born that way. He's accepted it. He's a great kid."

So, every time he was asked the question, Abbott's reply was the same. "I never told myself, 'I want to be the next Pete Gray,'" he repeatedly insisted. "I said, 'I want to be the next Nolan Ryan.'" He then would brace himself for another ques-

had done as many as 25 interviews and he was beginning to feel the strain. The Angels front office considered giving him a "stay-at-the-hotel day off" so he could take a break from the endless questioning. "But that would constitute sort of preferential treatment," Tim Mead feared, "and that's one thing we're trying to avoid."

Finally, Abbott went to Mead and asked for a two-day moratorium on interviews. He felt as if he were answering the questions by rote, without thinking. He needed some time away from the press so he could clear his mind and, more important, focus on baseball. When his two-day respite was up, Abbott welcomed back the army of reporters with a patient smile.

"He may be the most remarkable individual I've ever known in baseball," Rader said with genuine esteem. "It's been wearing at times. He's had to answer some of the dumbest, most undignified questions I've ever heard, but he's handled everything with dignity and grace."

The Japanese reporters came up with queries that never would have occurred to an American sports writer. They asked him things like, "What will be the first ball you throw against Seattle?"—imagine a major-league pitcher revealing that in advance—and, "What is your blood type?" But Abbott took it all in stride. "Theirs is a different culture," he said with an amused shrug.

In addition, many of the journalists who were assigned to cover the Abbott "story" were not sports writers, and they asked more than their share of naive and uninformed questions. And some questions set an all-time low, not just for stupidity— "Were you born a natural left-hander?"—but insensitivity— "Do you have any brothers or sisters that are deformed?"

Perhaps the most frequently asked question of the spring concerned a one-armed former player named Pete Gray.

tion, hoping that, for a change, it might have something to do with baseball.

Abbott's patience and cooperation charmed the normally jaded sports writers and won him a band of influential supporters. "The boys and girls of the press so love this guy," mused Scott Ostler, two months into the season, "it is almost embarrassing to him. This further complicates his life, since he is still trying to become a big-league pitcher and there isn't enough time to do all the baseball stuff *and* all the media stuff.

"What to do?" Ostler went on. "Turn hard-boiled and aloof? Hide out? He opts for Plan C: Learn to politely say no to the press, and pick his spots."

It wasn't easy, though, and the observant journalist could detect telltale signs of strain whenever the inevitable subject was raised. "When talk shifts from the left arm to the right," noted a 1987 *Sports Illustrated* profile, "Abbott's blue eyes dim and his blond head bows. He's not mad or annoyed, just once again reminded that he's stuck with this starring role straight out of a made-for-TV movie."

Claiming to be oblivious to the fuss, Abbott nevertheless did his best to draw the focus away from his condition. He frequently threw a towel over his right arm when television reporters come into the locker room, *Newsweek* reported in Abbott's rookie year, "and [he] tightens it nervously if the questions get too sappy."

"If I had two hands," the press-weary pitcher observed in early June, "there wouldn't be all this attention. I'd just be another left-handed pitcher." That's undoubtedly true. The trouble is, Jim Abbott will always be more than just another pitcher.

He is more than just another pitcher to Randy Sobek. Born with one hand, the four-and-a-half-year-old boy saw Abbott pitching on television in 1987. "Daddy!" he exclaimed with glee. "That boy has a special hand just like me!" After that day, his parents taped every televised game that Abbott pitched. "We keep the tape right by the TV," Randy's mother, Carol Sobek, explained, "and Randy watches it all the time, for inspiration." And Randy began practicing Abbott's hand-glove switch with his father. "I want to field just like he does when I play baseball or T-ball," Randy announced.

He is more than just another pitcher to Erin Bower. While shopping with her mother in April 1989, the five-year-old picked up a tube of toothpaste that someone had tampered with. The tube exploded, and Erin lost a hand. When Abbott heard about the horrible incident, he sent her a sensitive, reassuring letter. "I just won my first major-league game," he wrote. "When the final out was made, a lot of things went through my mind. . . . The only thing, Erin, that I didn't pay attention to was my handicap. You see, it had nothing to do with anything."

And he is more than just another pitcher to Laura Small. Mauled by a mountain lion in 1987 when she was seven, Laura suffered paralysis on her right side and lost the use of her right hand. "I want to be a doctor," she wrote to Abbott in 1989, "and seeing you makes me think I can be what I want to be." Abbott responded with praise and encouragement. "Remember," he told Laura, "our handicaps are only problems in the eyes of others."

Laura understood. "I think we have a lot in common," she told the *Los Angeles Times,* and mentioned how badly she felt that Abbott's disability had gotten so much attention. She also refused to discuss her attack anymore with reporters. "I'm so tired of being special!" Laura complained. "I just want to be ordinary!" How many times did Abbott feel like yelling those exact words in the middle of a postgame press conference or interview?

But early on, Abbott had learned to face reality. "I pitch to win," he once told a reporter, "not to be courageous. But I've grown up enough to know that being called a one-handed pitcher is not an insult. If it helps a kid or the parents of a kid in a similar situation, then I guess it makes my playing even more worthwhile. That goes beyond just baseball."

Just being there seems to help. Disabled kids flock to the ballpark whenever he is slated to start, whether at home or on the road. "I saw Abbott pitch three times in 1989," recalled baseball statistician-historian Bill James, "and each time seated near me I could see three or four little boys with a hand missing or some very similar condition. . . . There must have been two or three hundred in the park every time Abbott pitched, maybe more."

Realizing what he means to them, Abbott does whatever he can to establish a personal connection with these kids. Although he receives so much mail—sometimes up to 300 pieces a week—that the bulk of it has to be answered by the team's public relations department, Abbott responds to their letters personally, the way he did for Laura Small. And he quietly chats with them at whatever ballpark he is playing in.

Abbott described for *Sports Illustrated* one such occasion at Anaheim Stadium in 1991, when he visited in the Angels clubhouse with a seven-year-old boy who had only parts of two fingers on one hand. "He asks me," Abbott recounted, " 'Did kids ever tease you?' And it takes me back, because they did. . . . And he said, 'They called me Crab at camp.' A vicious thing, that is.

"So I said, 'Yeah, they teased me, too. Do you think it's a problem?' And he says, 'No.' I asked, 'Is there anything you can't do?' And he says, 'No.' And I said, 'Well, I don't think so either.' "

Clearly Abbott is more than a hero to children like this.

Heroes are remote, distant figures, mythic in their proportions, larger than life. Abbott, on the other hand, tries to be a real person to these kids. He is their counselor, role model, friend. Abbott reaches them because he knows them. He is all those disabled children that look up to him, and they are he. And so, these visits also seem to benefit Abbott, relieving his own feelings of self-doubt, reassuring him whenever he begins to wonder, "What am I doing here?"

"For the first time," Abbott continued, remembering that particular visit, "I said to somebody, 'Look at me, I'm playing with these guys. There's Dave Winfield and Dave Parker and Wally Joyner. I'm playing with them and I'm just like you.' And I don't know if it helps or not. . . . I don't even know if that's the point of it. But maybe it's just the fact that he has something to relate to."

The parents of disabled children also need something to relate to. They write to Abbott, thanking him for the example that he has set, although, he has maintained, "I think it's my parents these people should be talking to, not me." His mother and father, Abbott always insists, were his best role models.

"I can only imagine what it'd be like to have a wife who's pregnant," he has said, certainly thinking about his own parents. "There's so much hope and praying for a normal child, for he or she to live a normal life.

"If that doesn't happen, what a trauma that really must be—'What do we do now? What's the right role model?' They feel like there's no standard for their children." That is, until now.

Perhaps this was an unfair burden to lay on Abbott's shoulders, especially in his first year of professional baseball. It is hard enough for a rookie pitcher to make the team, even harder when he hasn't spent a day in the minors. But on top of it, he had to serve as baseball's designated human-interest story, the embodiment of someone else's idea of courage, a reluctant, but never unwilling, role model. All Abbott ever wanted to do was get hitters out and win ballgames.

"When people talk of me as an inspiration," he said in his rookie season, "there are some days when I can't take it. I get tired of it. . . . More and more, though, I've begun to realize that playing with one hand *is* different. It's not a negative, it hasn't hindered me, it's just changed a few things."

And that really is the point. It's not that Jim Abbott ever had to prove anything, except that he was a big-league-caliber pitcher, and that was clear early in his first spring training. But in so doing, he also has provided a valuable lesson, one that enriches not just the narrow arena of sports but the broader world of everyday life. Abbott has demonstrated that disability does not mean inability, that, as he likes to say, you are handicapped only in the eyes of others. As Doug Rader declared with due admiration, "Jim is the most *un*handicapped person I know."

6

∿○ Downs and Ups

The start of the 1990 spring training season was held up for 32 days when the baseball team owners locked the players out of the camps until the players' union agreed to a new contract. Meanwhile Jim Abbott, one of the last players on the Angels' 40-man roster who was still unsigned for the coming season, was engaged in contract negotiations of his own.

As a rookie in 1989, Abbott earned the minimum major-league salary of $68,000. Because of his successful year on the field and his popularity with the fans, who turned out in droves whenever he pitched, Abbott and his agent, Scott Boras, thought he deserved a big raise. They asked for approximately $270,000, close to what Baltimore Orioles reliever Gregg Olson, the 1989 American League Rookie of the Year, had received. The Angels answered with a much lower offer, which Abbott and Boras refused.

In mid-March, with the camps still closed, the team increased its offer to $185,000. Abbott signed, but Boras seethed. "I am shocked," the agent declared. "This is not a great public relations move for the Angels. . . . Jim's first start drew over 100 members of the media. Every time he pitched, he drew over 5,000 extra fans. That's a lot of money for the Angels." True enough, but a 172 percent raise is a lot of money for a second-year pitcher.

Boras also implied that the Angels' hard stance could push his client into free agency once he became eligible. "Jim Abbott turned down millions in endorsements," he argued, "to devote his life to his baseball career. His motivation was entirely baseball. It's difficult for him not to receive a contract rewarding him for that sacrifice."

But while his agent talked tough—which, of course, is what agents do—Abbott was conciliatory. He admitted being disappointed in the team's offer, but once training camp finally opened, he vowed to put his feelings aside. "I really enjoy the camaraderie here," he said, "and I'd hate to carry something over from the off-season." Abbott also maintained that, despite Boras's veiled threat, he was not thinking about free agency. "If I'm fortunate enough to have a career that lasts that long," he insisted, "I'll cross that bridge when I come to it."

Abbott's first spring training appearance in 1990 was a huge, and welcome, change from the media circus of his rookie year. As he took the mound for the first time, he drew polite applause from the small crowd of 2,433. There were no camera crews and only the usual postgame interviews, but no press conference. Apparently the fuss had subsided, and that was fine with him. Abbott hoped that now he could concentrate on refining his skills and learning more about the craft of pitching in the major leagues.

Many casual baseball fans assume that the best way for a

pitcher to get hitters out is to blow fastball after fastball by them. But this strategy has one fatal flaw: over the course of a game, or sometimes in a single at bat, a good major-league hitter can adjust the timing of his swing to even the fastest fastball. Should that happen, and bat connects solidly with ball, the sheer force of the swing can turn the force of the pitch back in the opposite direction and send it flying out of the ballpark.

Abbott's major project for the spring was to develop an effective change-of-pace pitch, or "change-up," to go with his fastball and slider. A pitcher normally throws the change-up with the same motion he uses for his fastball. However, he grips the ball differently so that it will travel eight to 10 miles an hour slower. The hitter, expecting a fastball, will speed up his bat and end up swinging ahead of the pitch, which usually results in either a weakly batted ball or, even better, a strike. And so, the change-up is an effective weapon because it deceives the batter and throws off his timing.

Abbott also set two modest goals for the upcoming season: to win 15 games and improve his performance against left-handed hitters. Right-handed batters hit for a .263 average against Abbott, a slugging average of .361, and an on-base percentage of .335, numbers that were similar to his fellow Angels lefty, Chuck Finley (.243 BA, .356 SA, .320 OBP). Left-handed hitters, however, batted .325 against Abbott, with considerably more power (.463 SA) and a better on-base frequency (.388 OBP). Compare these figures to Finley's numbers against lefty hitters—.172 BA, .252 SA, .192 OBP—and the discrepancy simply screams out.

As a left-hander, Abbott should have enjoyed the kind of natural advantage over lefty batters that Finley displayed. However, his best pitch, the hard slider, was more effective against right-handers, breaking in on their fists, than left-handers. If he could master the change-up and improve his curveball, Abbott should be able to handle lefty hitters in a similar fashion.

Hoping to improve on the team's third-place finish in 1989, the Angels front office signed free-agent left-handed pitcher Mark Langston during the off season. This move strengthened an already-strong pitching staff and temporarily gave California six starters on the roster. The odd man out, Mike Witt, began the year in the bullpen, but was traded to the Yankees in May for Dave Winfield, one of the game's premier hitters. The Angels' management, players, and fans hoped that these two key acquisitions would put the team over the top in 1990.

But there are some things you can't account for during the off-season. By early June, the Angel roster was riddled by injuries, as well as weak hitting, and the team languished in sixth place. In mid-May their best young player, first baseman Wally Joyner, was hit on the right kneecap by a pitch. He played in pain for two months, until diagnosed with a stress fracture, and was out for the second half of the season. Pitcher Bert Blyleven, the 1989 American League Comeback Player of the Year, missed about a dozen starts because of a muscle strain in his right shoulder, and when he did pitch, he was ineffective.

By early August, the situation was desperate, and manager Doug Rader knew that better than anyone. "I think the team's mood is somewhere between asleep and frantic," he lamented. The Angels never got on track, limping to a fourth-place, 80-82 finish, 23 games behind the defending world champion Oakland Athletics.

It was a frustrating season for Abbott as well, who finished with a disappointing 10-14 record, which was not entirely his fault. The 1990 Angels were not a good hitting team, and they did not provide Abbott with much offensive support. His teammates scored only 4.08 runs per every nine innings Abbott pitched, slightly below the league average of 4.35. (Langston, who was 10-17, got even less support, 3.91 runs per nine innings.)

But on the whole, Abbott did not pitch all that well. He led the American Leagues in hits allowed (246). His ERA was a worrisome 4.51—4.93 if you add the unearned runs scored against him—which was well up from his rookie level. And he allowed 13.5 base runners per nine innings pitched, slightly worse than his 1989 figure.

Abbott had wanted to be more effective against left-handed batters, but any improvement was marginal, at best. Lefties hit .318 against him, with a slugging average of .436 and a .400 on-base percentage. And his numbers against right-handed hitters actually worsened—.292 BA, .396 SA, .346 OBP.

There were, however, some bright spots. For one thing, Abbott showed better control. In 1989 he walked 74 hitters in 181⅓ innings, while in 1990 he yielded 72 walks in 211⅔ innings. He also became more adept at holding runners on base. In his second season, Abbott was stolen on 15 times, an average of .64 stolen bases per every nine innings, a vast improvement over his previous year's mark (1.44).

Pitching coach Marcel Lachemann thus felt that 1990 represented "a step forward" for Abbott. "The numbers may not indicate it," the coach argued, "but he was improving on some things, holding the runners, throwing the outside pitch. It was progress."

Abbott was disappointed in his 1990 performance, but he tried to focus on the positives. "I think I've had a better year than some of my statistics show," he observed. "I had some lousy games, and I'm the first to admit that. . . . But I've worked hard and I'm proud of what I've done. I think I'm a better pitcher and next year I'll be even better."

"There are a lot of things I've learned," he continued, "like getting a much better idea of what to throw and when to throw it. . . . I know the hitters better and the league better and how to pace myself through the season."

In other words, Abbott was making the slow, but necessary, evolution from "thrower" to "pitcher." As a hot-stuff college baseball star, all he had to do was rear back, heave the ball at the plate, and blow the hitters away, one after another. But in the big leagues, a pitcher must plan ahead, mix up his pitches, change speeds, and move the ball around the strike zone.

Lance Parrish believed that Abbott, despite the tough season, had made strong progress in that direction. "Instead of just pitching to people," the catcher argued, "he was thinking about how to set people up with certain pitches. He hit both corners [of the plate] with his curveball a little better and he has the change-up. When he polishes the things he's trying to accomplish this year, like hitting the outside corner, I think his record will improve dramatically." Parrish predicted 17 to 19 wins for Abbott in 1991.

Why not 20 wins, then? "Could I win 20 games?" Abbott reflected. "It takes a lot of things to win 20. I think I can be a good pitcher and contribute positively to a contending team. That would be my goal."

Most of all, it was a far more peaceful year for Abbott. He was "old news," and glad of it. There were fewer demands for interviews and personal appearances, and he had more time to relax and focus on his job. Still, he spent as much time as ever visiting with disabled children.

In 1990, the Angels front office had hoped to improve the club by signing Mark Langston and trading for Dave Winfield. In 1991, it hoped to improve the club by hiring "sports psychologist" Ken Ravizza. It was a sign of the times. Imagine Ty Cobb or Babe Ruth or Ted Williams consulting a psychologist during a batting slump. Ravizza would be in charge of positive thinking, self-image, dealing with pressure, and goal setting.

There would be some new faces on the field, as well. The front office acquired a pair of veterans, third baseman Gary Gaetti and designated hitter Dave Parker, and a promising youngster, outfielder Junior Felix. They would be in charge of scoring more runs.

The highlight of Abbott's 1991 spring training camp came in a late-March exhibition game against the San Francisco Giants in Scottsdale, Arizona. Abbott, who had batted only seven times since high school, smacked a 375-foot triple into right-center field, his first hit in a major-league uniform. And just like a pitcher, he still was crowing about it far into the season. "He will suggest," wrote Hank Hersch in a September profile for *Sports Illustrated*, "that there is not enough tape in a reporter's recorder to cover a discussion of the triple he hit in spring training."

On the mound, however, there was not much for Abbott to brag about that spring—no wins, three losses, a 5.02 ERA. But that was just practice. After all, your spring training numbers can't predict how you'll do once the real season begins, right?

Well maybe, except that Abbott also lost each of his first four regular-season outings. Although his ERA during that stretch was a surprisingly high 6.00, Abbott's 0-4 start was not entirely his fault. With a little help from the Angels hitters, he might have won at least two of those games. However, California scored just seven runs in Abbott's four April losses: 6-0, 3-1, 4-3, 7-3. "I'm too big to cry about it," the pitcher said, paraphrasing his hero, Abraham Lincoln, "but it hurts too much to laugh."

By the end of the season's first month, fair-weather fans

from all over Southern California were jamming the phone lines at the call-in sports talk shows, criticizing Abbott and demanding that he be sent down to the minors. "It was all about pitching—," he observed, "this guy stinks. I thought, 'There it is. Finally. I've arrived.' " For the first time, Abbott was being talked about, not as a hero or an inspiration, but solely as a pitcher.

Still, the talk was largely negative, and Abbott found it frustrating. To Marcel Lachemann, it was insulting. Strange as it may seem, it is not unusual for a team's front office to be influenced by the prattle of these "experts," who can spout their opinions for the cost of a local phone call. But no matter what, Lachemann resolved to stick by his pitcher. As far as he was concerned, Abbott belonged in the major leagues and there he would stay. "I told him, 'I'll sink or swim with you,' " the coach revealed. "It may cost me my job, but they'll have to send us both out."

Later in the season, Abbott admitted that the slump and all the negative talk surrounding it brought back those old feelings of self-doubt. "It was the toughest thing I've gone through, ballwise, in a long time," he recalled. "In the back of your mind you think, 'Maybe I just don't have it.' . . . And then all of a sudden, your worst fears are out in the open, in public debate.

"I know a lot of people said that because of my hand, I had something to prove. I never felt that was the case. For some reason, I have a real dislike for the adamant, 'I'm going to *prove* something.' But I felt I wanted to vindicate the people who had helped me."

And he did get plenty of help. Lachemann advised Abbott to work inside to the hitters, stop trying to nibble with the off-speed stuff, and rely on his power pitches, the hard slider and the cut fastball. Ravizza, the team psychologist, taught Abbott to relax by giving him a mantra to say to himself on the mound: "Trust it, trust it, you've been here before." He received sympathetic pats on the back from his teammates, encouraging phone calls from his parents in Flint, a sense of security from his fiancée, Dana Douty.

The slump, and all the mindless criticism, finally ended on May 5, when Abbott won his first game of the year, a 6-4 decision over the Baltimore Orioles. He was pleased with the win but not with his performance—eight hits, three walks, three earned runs, and just two strikeouts in five and two-thirds innings. "If we score six runs every game that'll turn it around," the self-critical pitcher remarked. "Today was my worst game of the year, to be honest."

At least this time Abbott received some on-field support from his teammates. In the Angels' six-run fourth inning, Gary Gaetti hit a three-run homer and Luis Polonia contributed a two-run triple. The night before, Polonia placed his lucky doll, Joe Vu, in Abbott's locker. "I may steal it before my next start," the pitcher laughed.

But Abbott no longer needed good-luck charms. From the Oriole game to the All-Star break, he won seven and lost two, with a 2.78 ERA. Meanwhile, Angels left-handers Mark Langston and Chuck Finley, who had started the season hot and never cooled down, were both 12-3 at the break. Overall, the Angels were sitting in third place at the halfway point with a 44-37 record, two games behind the Texas Rangers and the Minnesota Twins, who were tied for first in the American League West.

As the 1991 season wound through its second half, Abbott showed no signs of letting up. "Several times I've seen him with legitimate no-hit stuff," Gary Gaetti said prophetically, "where nobody's come close to attacking the ball."

Eleven-year-old Little Leaguer, Jim Abbott. *Flint Journal Photo.*

Flint Central quarterback Jim Abbott hands the ball off. "I honestly feel . . . he could have been a quarterback at the college level," Abbott's high school football coach insisted. *Flint Journal Photo.*

Jim at 16, star of the Flint Grossi Connie Mack League team, flanked by his proud parents, Kathy and Mike Abbott. *Flint Journal Photo.*

Abbott enjoyed a tremendous senior year at Flint Central High School—10-3, 0.76 ERA, 148 strikeouts in 73 innings, and four no-hitters (including a perfect game). *Flint Journal Photo*.

On the mound during Team USA's 18-0 trouncing of Nicaragua at the 1987 Pan American Games. *UPI/Bettmann.*

Abbott and Team USA teammate Dave Silvestri are ecstatic after winning the gold medal at the 1988 Summer Olympics. *UPI/Bettmann.*

Abbott loves to talk about his supposed batting prowess. Through three years at Michigan, he hit .667 (two for three), and in 1991 he had a spring training triple that he still was bragging about in September. ©1990 *Jeff Carlick, Sportschrome East/West.*

Straight to the big leagues—Abbott as a 21-year-old California Angels rookie. *Flint Journal Photo.*

"How about that, baby!" Jim Abbott and Yankees teammate Wade Boggs celebrate Abbott's no-hitter over Cleveland, September 4, 1993. *Reuters/Bettmann.*

A frustrated Abbott sweats out a tough August 1993 loss. He pitched well enough to win, but his Yankees teammates grounded into four double plays and left seven runners in scoring position. Final score: Texas 4, New York 2. *Reuters/Bettmann.*

Abbott had become a complete pitcher. "Last year, he was one-dimensional," catcher Lance Parrish observed. Now, instead of throwing his fastball to the same spot most of the time, Abbott was moving his pitches around the strike zone, and that, Parrish felt, made all the difference.

Unfortunately, the Angels never got it going in the second half, and on August 26, Doug Rader was fired as manager and replaced by Buck Rodgers. Marcel Lachemann remained as pitching coach. One week later, a new general manager, Whitey Herzog, was hired to rebuild the team for 1992. It was too late to do anything about 1991. Just over a month later, the Angels finished the year at 81-81, the best record ever for a last-place club.

As the season came to a close, Abbott was being spoken of as a Cy Young Award candidate. "It's ridiculous," he insisted. "It never entered my mind." Nevertheless, his 18-11 record (11-5 since the All-Star break) and 2.89 ERA were enough to place him third in the voting.

In fact, Abbott pitched even better than his stellar won-lost record indicated. He struck out 158 batters, a career high, and his strikeout-walk ratio was 2.16, which, for the first time in three seasons, was above the league average (1.67). He reduced his base runners per nine innings pitched to 10.9 and allowed just 12 stolen bases in 243 innings, an average of .44 per nine innings.

Abbott's record was even more impressive, considering that he frequently was let down by the Angels' bullpen and hitters. On four occasions, he left the game with a lead and a potential victory, only to see the relief pitcher blow it. And on the whole, he enjoyed only fair offensive support, an average of 4.70 runs per nine innings, slightly above the league average (4.49).

Author Bill James evaluates how well a pitcher has performed in a particular outing by calculating what he calls a "game score." The game score is based on the pitcher's statistical performance, that is, the number of batters retired, innings completed, strikeouts, walks, hits, and runs, both earned and unearned, for that game. An average game score is 50.

From this starting point, James went on to develop the concept of "tough losses." A tough loss is any game in which a starting pitcher is charged with a defeat despite a game score of 50 or better, in other words, an above-average performance. James figured that, in 1991, Abbott led the American League in "tough losses," with eight. Although he was 0-8 in those games, Abbott lasted an average of almost eight innings per start with an overall ERA of 2.97.

There were some real heartbreakers, like his 2-0 complete-game loss to the Yankees on July 13, and his 1-0 complete-game defeat against the White Sox on September 13. (One needn't bother asking how Abbott felt about the number 13.) In both of those outings his game score was 72, well above average.

On September 24, Abbott pitched what may have been the best game of his career to that point. Through nine innings he had shut out the always-tough Toronto Blue Jays, holding them to two hits and walking none. Meanwhile, Blue Jays starter Todd Stottlemyre and reliever David Wells were doing the same thing to the Angels. The game went into extra innings deadlocked 0-0.

Candy Maldonado opened the Toronto half of the tenth with a single and moved to second on John Olerud's sacrifice fly. With first base open, manager Buck Rodgers ordered Abbott to walk Pat Tabler intentionally, setting up the possibility of an inning-ending double play. The strategy backfired when the next batter, Pat Borders, hit Abbott's first pitch into the left-field seats for a three-run homer. Abbott struck out the following two hitters, but the damage had been done.

The Angels failed to score in the bottom of the inning, and Abbott was hung with his toughest defeat of the year. In 10 innings he had struck out 13 and given up just four hits and that intentional walk. His game score was a brilliant 84, but he still lost, 3-0. "A loss is a loss," Abbott reflected sadly. "They hurt whether they're by seven or by one."

The 1991 Angels were a baseball anomaly. Their three top starters, lefties Langston, Finley, and Abbott, posted won-lost records of 19-8, 18-9, and 18-11, respectively, as good as any three pitchers on any one team in baseball that season. Reliever Bryan Harvey led the league in saves, with 46. (Abbott and Harvey were honored as the team's co-MVPs.) With that kind of front-line pitching, the Angels should have been contenders for the division title.

The problem was offense—there simply wasn't any. Only Wally Joyner hit above .300 (.301). Overall the Angels ranked next to last in the American League in runs scored, home runs, slugging average, and on-base percentage. It also was an old team. Four of the regulars were over 30—Gaetti (31), Parrish (35), Winfield (40), and Parker (40)—and for most of these veterans, their best seasons were behind them. Changes would have to be made.

Luckily, the new general manager, Whitey Herzog, was just the guy to make them. In 1980, as the St. Louis Cardinals' newly hired general manager, Herzog arrived at baseball's winter meetings and began dealing. He traded away 13 players and acquired nine new ones, including relief ace Bruce Sutter, and signed one free agent, catcher Darrell Porter. Then, during the 1981 off-season, Herzog traded for outfielders Lonnie Smith and Willie McGee and shortstop Ozzie Smith. In 1982, Herzog's rebuilt Cardinals won the World Series.

Could Herzog do the same for the California Angels?

Possibly, but it would require more than savvy trades. The kind of large-scale rebuilding program that the Angels needed meant signing high-quality free agents, and that would cost money. And therein lay Herzog's problem.

At age 84, owner Gene Autry no longer handled the decision making for the Angels organization. The once free-spending cowboy had ceded total control to his wife, Jackie, a 50-year-old former banker. "We have the nucleus of a good ball-club that was put together correctly," she told the *Sporting News* in September, "and if we can add some players in the right places, I think we can be a very good ballclub." It appeared as if she would give Herzog the green light, if not carte blanche, to do whatever was necessary to improve the team.

However, in that same interview, Autry announced that the team would lose an estimated $2 million in 1991 and would thus have to tighten its belt. "We have to reduce the payroll if we want to remain financially viable," she maintained. It was a clear and ominous message to the new general manager: there will be no more open-checkbook forays into the free-agent market for the California Angels.

The Angels had their own free-agent players to worry about. Herzog managed to re-sign Chuck Finley to a four-year contract, and was hoping to keep Kirk McCaskill, the number-four starter who, Herzog believed, pitched better than his 10-19 record indicated. "We scored only two runs or less in 14 of his 19 losses," the GM noted. "We want him back." McCaskill, however, eventually signed with the Chicago White Sox.

Most important of all, there was Wally Joyner, the Angels' best everyday player. A history of bitter negotiations and two salary arbitration hearings, both of which were won by Joyner, had created animosity between Joyner and Jackie Autry. Herzog offered the first baseman a total of $15.75 million for the next four seasons. Joyner wanted $9.75 million over the first two years of the deal, but Jackie Autry insisted on limiting it to $9 million.

In early December, it appeared as if Herzog were close to signing the first baseman, but negotiations broke down. Herzog gave Joyner a 48-hour deadline to agree to a contract. Joyner finally signed—a one-year, $4.2 million deal with the Kansas City Royals.

Herzog had hoped to bolster the Angels' anemic lineup by signing blue-chip free-agent outfielders Otis Nixon (.297 batting average, 72 stolen bases) and Bobby Bonilla (.302, 18 home runs, 100 RBIs), who would have batted leadoff and cleanup, respectively. He could not come up with enough money, however, and these all-star-caliber players went to other teams. Once those deals fell through, there was talk about signing free-agent outfielder Danny Tartabull, but that's all it was—talk.

Instead, Herzog traded for two injury-prone, over-30 players, Von Hayes (33 years old) and Hubie Brooks (35). Both new Angels were coming off the worst batting average seasons of their careers. Hayes hit .225 in just 77 games in 1991, while Brooks, who missed the last seven weeks of the schedule, batted .238.

In December, Herzog looked at his 1992 California Angels roster with resignation. "The Cowboy has waited 30 years for a pennant," he said, referring to Gene Autry's decades of frustration. "I hope he can wait 31." Herzog didn't have to say what was brutally clear to everyone: Jackie Autry's tightfisted policy was the reason that, come next September, the old singing cowboy's canteen still would be empty.

In early January, Herzog tried to put together a deal to keep Jim Abbott on the team for the next three seasons but was unable to come to terms with the pitcher and his agent, Boras.

Under the collective bargaining agreement between the baseball owners and the players' union, Abbott, as a three-year major-league player, was eligible to demand a salary arbitration hearing as the means of resolving the impasse.

At such a hearing, representatives of the player and the team meet before an impartial arbitrator, who functions much like a judge. Each side states a salary figure for the upcoming season and presents an argument as to why that amount is a fair one. The arbitrator listeners to the cases and then rules in favor of one side or the other. That decision is final, and both parties are bound by it.

Abbott, who made $357,500 in 1991, was seeking $2.1 million for 1992. The Angels were offering $1.6 million, which would make him the highest-paid fourth-year pitcher in baseball history. They were about to go to arbitration when, in late January, Abbott and Boras suggested splitting the difference. The Angels agreed and Abbott signed a one-year contract worth $1.85 million.

Even though the matter never went to a hearing, Abbott benefited from the system. Because the arbitrator must select either the team's offer or the player's request, both parties have to keep their figures reasonable. If the player asks for an exorbitantly inflated salary, the arbitrator will rule against him. Likewise, if the team tries to make a low-ball bid, the arbitrator will side with the player. Consequently, the Angels offered Abbott more than they otherwise would have. "Without arbitration," Herzog admitted in a *Sporting News* debate on the subject, "we probably would have signed Abbott for a little over a million."

Abbott was delighted that the matter could be resolved so easily, and he spoke about playing in Anaheim in the years to come. "If the Angels want me around on a long-term basis," the fan favorite said with genuine hope, "that would be terrific." Abbott liked living in Southern California and was putting down roots there. He and Dana Douty, who grew up in Fountain Valley, California, near Anaheim, were married in December, and they had a home in the nearby town of Newport Beach.

Abbott enjoyed his best spring yet in 1992, posting a 2-1 record with a 2.86 ERA, striking out 23 batters and walking only 9 in 22⅓ innings. Again he pondered his chances of winning 20 games in the upcoming season. His performance in 1991 taught Abbott two things: that he had the ability to win 20 and that winning 20 requires more than just ability.

"You can pitch very well and not get good results," he observed in mid-March, "and get discouraged if you don't win. And if you're throwing poorly and get good results, you can say, 'I'm OK,' and run into trouble later. Every pitcher would love to win 20, but it takes a lot of luck."

The signs may have been good for Abbott, but for the Angels it was another matter. Herzog still hoped to boost the team's weak offense and in February signed first baseman–DH Alvin Davis, another 30-something player coming off the worst year of his career (12 home runs, .221 batting average). Given the financial constraints under which he had to work, this was the best that Herzog could do.

Toward the end of spring training, Jackie Autry met with reporters in Palm Springs. She revealed that the California Angels lost $3.6 million dollars in 1991—$1.6 million more than she originally estimated—and projected an $8.5 million loss for 1992. If the situation did not change, Autry threatened, she would be forced to sell the team, claiming that, even if the Angels made the playoffs and the World Series in 1992, the club still would lose money.

As Opening Day neared, Herzog looked at the job he

had done over the winter. "We can't hit and we can't run," he said soberly, "and that makes it tough on a manager when he has to wait for those three-run homers." It also makes it tough on a team when it has to hear that kind of talk, however realistic it may be, from its general manager before the season has even begun.

One early-season game, on April 29 in Toronto, suggested the kind of year it would be for Abbott. For eight innings he pitched shutout ball, scattering six hits and three walks and striking out seven. Meanwhile, Blue Jays starter Todd Stottlemyre had shut out the Angels on seven hits. It was a classic 0-0 pitchers' duel.

With two out in the bottom of the ninth, Abbott allowed back-to-back singles. Pat Borders's bouncer to third should have ended the inning, but the ball rolled off Gary Gaetti's glove for an error, loading the bases and prolonging the threat. Then it all fell apart. Abbott's control abandoned him and he walked Pat Tabler to force home the winning run. His "game score" for this mind-numbing 1-0 loss was 67.

As the game reached its gruesome end, Abbott, perplexed and dazed, stood on the mound, staring at home plate. Afterward, Buck Rodgers tried to console his pitcher. "This is the toughest game you're going to lose," the manager told him. "You may pitch for 20 years and not lose a tougher one than that."

Through his first 11 starts in 1992, Abbott had won two and lost seven, but his ERA was an excellent 2.75. The problem lay not in his pitching but in his team's lack of hitting. The Angels scored an average of just 2.09 runs per nine innings in Abbott's starts, the lowest offensive support for any pitcher in the American League. In other words, Abbott couldn't have pitched much better, but his team let him down almost every time he took the mound.

"I have to find rewards other than winning and losing," he explained. "That's the way a pitcher is judged, but I have to find other ways to save my confidence. Right now, it's running a little low."

By early June, the Angels' record was 22-32, and Abbott could see his teammates' frustration and lack of confidence. "We know we're playing bad baseball," he said. "We know we're down. . . . The breaks of the game are going against us. If we can turn that around, and a few things go right, then the confidence kicks in, and you win some ballgames." The 24-year-old pitcher was speaking like a team leader. Unfortunately, he was a leader on a bad team.

By the All-Star break, Abbott's record had fallen to 4-11, even though his 2.96 ERA placed him among the league leaders. "You know it hurts," he admitted in the clubhouse after another tough loss. "But what am I going to do, come in here and throw things around? . . . I can't let this affect me. I'm just going to keep going out there every five days and do the best I can."

It is not surprising that Abbott's misfortunes mirrored those of his team. Thanks to weak hitting, bad breaks, and an 11-game losing streak, the Angels hit midseason with a 35-52 record. "But it's still pretty early," Abbott continued optimistically. "If any team can rebound, it's this one."

If Abbott believed that, he was fooling himself. The 1992 California Angels simply did not possess enough talent to mount a second-half drive. The sort of players that might have made a run for the pennant possible—1991 free agents like Wally Joyner, Bobby Bonilla, Otis Nixon, and Danny Tartabull—all had ended up playing elsewhere.

In late July, Abbott went on the disabled list with a pulled back muscle, causing him to miss some starts. The injury was not serious, however, and other teams were expressing interest in him. The Blue Jays reportedly wanted Abbott to bolster their ultimately successful stretch drive. The New York tabloids and call-in shows reported rumors of a three-for-one trade that would have put Abbott in Yankees pinstripes.

Herzog claimed that he had taken calls from five general managers regarding a possible deal for Abbott, but he wasn't interested, at least not yet. "We're not going to trade Abbott," Herzog maintained. "We're trying to sign him [to a multiyear contract]. If I see that can't be done, then we're going to have to make a deal."

Marcel Lachemann lamented the fact that Abbott, who by this point was 5-12, now had to deal with these added distractions. "The won-loss record is obviously on his mind," Lachemann noted, "but every other day there are trade rumors, and I guess he's got contract negotiations going on, too. A lot of things could take his concentration away, but when he goes out there between the lines, his competitive nature takes over."

As always, Abbott appreciated Lachemann's support but was somewhat amused by his coach's comments. "I guess you could say I've been distracted by contract negotiations if any were going on," he said with uncharacteristic sarcasm, "but they're not. We had one meeting, and they said they wanted to sign me, and I haven't heard much since."

At least one other Angels player, Lance Parrish, wondered what the team was doing to secure Abbott for the future. "It seems like every time Jackie [Autry] says something in the paper, it has to do with money," Parrish remarked in early September, "so that obviously has a lot to do with the decisions that they're trying to make over here. I would think if money had nothing to do with it, they would have signed Jim Abbott to a multiyear deal by now."

The California Angels' 1992 season came to a painful end with the club tied for fifth place with Kansas City, 24 games behind division-leading Oakland. The team's 72-90 record was its worst since 1983, and it finished last in the American League in batting average, slugging average, and on-base percentage.

Although Abbott's final won-lost record was 7-15, his other stats were as good, if not better, than those in his 18-win season of a year ago. He struck out 130 hitters in 211 innings, walking 68. His 2.77 ERA was the fifth best in the American League and his lowest ever, and from the All-Star break to the end of the season he posted a 2.45 ERA, the second lowest in the league over that stretch. Despite missing some starts in the second half, Abbott threw seven complete games, another personal best. And he almost won the league fielding title for pitchers, handling 46 chances without an error, second best in the league.

In his previous three seasons with California, Abbott seldom enjoyed strong offensive support. In 1989, the Angels were outscored 65-23 in his 12 losses and scored one or zero runs six times. The following year, the team scored a total of just 15 runs in Abbott's 14 losses. And in 1991, they scored 20 runs in his 11 losses.

But 1992 was his all-time low. The Angels scored three runs or fewer in 24 of Abbott's 29 starts and averaged just 2.55 runs per game. Not only was that the lowest run-support figure for any starting pitcher in the American League in 1992, it was the lowest in the American League since the advent of the designated-hitter rule in 1973 and the lowest in Angels history. Abbott was the Robinson Crusoe of baseball, stranded every five days on that tiny dirt island called a pitcher's mound, surviving by his wits alone with not even a faithful Friday to supply the occasional game-winning hit.

So how well did Abbott *really* pitch in 1992? Bill James devised a series of formulas that make it possible to adjust Abbott's 1992 won-lost record by taking into account his meager offensive support. Applying James's system, if Abbott had received average support that year (4.34 runs per game for the American League), he could have finished with a record of at least 14-9, rather than 7-15.

Of course, this is all highly speculative. In the real world, Jim Abbott won seven games and lost 15 in 1992, and no amount of statistical manipulation will erase or alter these hard facts. The point here is merely to show that Abbott, having allowed an average of just 3.11 runs (earned plus unearned) per nine innings that season, actually pitched much better than his won-lost record indicated.

With the record books closed on 1992, the Angels front office turned its attention to the task of signing their hard-luck starter to a multiyear contract. Herzog offered to pay Abbott a total of $16 million over the next four years, which would have made him the highest-paid four-year pitcher in history. Abbott and Boras countered by asking for $19 million. When Herzog balked at their figure, the pitcher and his agent suggested splitting the difference, as they did the previous winter, but the Angels general manager held fast to his initial offer.

And so, in October, the negotiations between Abbott and the Angels hit an impasse. Other teams were interested in him, and there were trade rumors involving the Blue Jays and the Yankees. But as December neared, the Abbotts left for a Hawaiian vacation. Abbott was confident that the contract differences would eventually be resolved and that he would be back in friendly Anaheim for the 1993 season.

Returning from their trip, the couple was met at the airport by Dana's mother. "Have you heard?" she asked her daughter and son-in-law. "Heard what?" they replied. "You've been traded." Jim Abbott, the Angels' most popular player, would be exchanging his halo for pinstripes—*New York Yankee* pinstripes.

7

∼o Yankee

"This is my deal," Whitey Herzog told the press after the Angels traded Jim Abbott to the Yankees for three minor-league prospects, first baseman J. T. Snow, right-handed starting pitcher Russ Springer, and lefty reliever Jerry Nielsen. "I take full responsibility."

Since the end of the season, the Angels general manager had been engaged in constant negotiations with other teams, trying to trade Abbott. Some seven or eight clubs expressed an interest in acquiring the pitcher. Herzog narrowed down the finalists to the White Sox, Twins, Expos, and Yankees, before finally accepting New York's offer. "I'd talked to [Yankees general manager] Gene Michael more than I had my wife the last couple of months," he joked. So in that sense, at least, this was Herzog's deal.

However, given the economic constraints under which he was forced to operate, it was not Herzog's deal at all, as he all but admitted. "It boiled down to waiting for the Cowboy [owner Gene Autry] to come in," the general manager explained. "He thought a lot of Jim Abbott, and so do I. But this is something we felt we had to do, and we still have to do more."

In other words, all Herzog needed was the approval of Gene Autry—that is to say, *Jackie* Autry, who controlled the organization's purse strings—and he might have signed Abbott to the four-year, $17.5 million compromise deal that the pitcher and his agent had suggested. But Gene Autry's admiration for Abbott counted for nothing next to Jackie Autry's three-word directive to Herzog: cut the payroll. And so, unloading Abbott and his salary demands was what, as Herzog said, "we had to do."

Since the start of the 1992 season, the Angels had already cut nearly $20 million in player salaries. For example, reliever Bryan Harvey, with his three-year, $10.75 million contact, was left unprotected in the expansion draft and scooped up by the Florida Marlins. (In 1991, he and Abbott had been the Angels' co-MVPs.) Harvey recovered from the elbow problems that sidelined him for part of the 1992 season and saved 45 games for Florida in 1993.

Why couldn't some of that money have gone toward keeping Abbott with the Angels? Was it earmarked for some other purpose, like signing a quality free agent, for a change? Apparently not. Herzog pursued Paul Molitor, but the lifetime .301 hitter signed with Toronto (where he batted .332, hitting 22 homers with 111 RBIs in 1993). No other worthwhile free agents were added to the Angels' roster during the off-season.

The Abbott trade finally drove home what, for the past year, was becoming painfully evident: building a winner was no longer the primary goal of the Angels' ownership. Valuable, young stars, like Harvey and Wally Joyner, were cut loose. Free-agent signings were measly and anticlimactic. Now, the team's most popular player was traded for three minor-leaguer prospects who, if they made the club, would earn no more than the minimum major-league salary of $109,000 each.

Jackie Autry, as sports writer Dave Cunningham once observed, "knows that the best way to make money from baseball is to sell a club." Time and again, she had announced her intention to put the Angels on the market. With its shrunken payroll, the franchise would be more attractive to whatever potential buyers she might drum up. (The San Diego Padres were pursuing a similar course, letting go of all their best, and highest-priced, players, with the sole exception of the great hitter Tony Gwynn.) Without Abbott, not to mention Joyner and Harvey, the Angels were going to look a lot better on the balance sheet in 1993 than they would on the field.

The Abbott trade illustrates the kind of "bottom line" thinking that is anathema to a real baseball man like Herzog. Experience had taught him that winning teams are built by spending money, spending it wisely, of course, but nevertheless spending it. But this was something that the Angels' ownership was no longer willing to do. By the winter of 1993–94, Herzog, fed up with this no-win situation, resigned from the Angels' front office.

That Abbott had fallen victim to Jackie Autry's austerity scheme was an indisputable fact that few observers could miss. "It's sad that this has come to be such a business that we have to trade Jim Abbott," Bert Blyleven lamented, speaking for the rest of his Angels teammates. "But we as players knew going into the winter meetings, the Angels were going to trade Jim Abbott because they couldn't sign him."

"We're going to take heat for this," an anonymous club

official predicted, "big-time heat." He was right—one local newspaper polled its readers about the trade and elicited an unfavorable reaction from 98 percent of the respondents.

Naturally, the Los Angeles writers skewered the Angels front office for dumping the fan—and press—favorite. Jim Abbott is "a pitcher with a proven record and a heroic story," declared Ross Newhan in the *Los Angeles Times*. Like so many other popular Angels players before him, he was dealt away, Newhan wrote, "with no apparent concern for the cost in public relations."

Two months later, the sting remained sharp. "I have never enjoyed watching a baseball player as much as I've enjoyed watching Jim Abbott," wrote the *Los Angeles Times*'s Mike Downey in February, expressing the writers' consensus. "Many others feel the same way. I never thought the Angels would let him go, and I think they will rue the day they did."

Downey also discovered an interesting and ironic twist to the story. "The one thing Jim Abbott wanted was to be treated like any other player," he observed. "And so he was. Traded away, even though he was one of Gene Autry's most valuable players and undoubtedly the most popular. . . . Dependable as anyone. Expendable as anyone."

Of course, no one was more stunned by the trade than Abbott himself. "It's been a tough day for me," he commented immediately after it happened. Abbott's clipped, repetitive sentences seemed to embody his sorrow and disillusionment. "It's been an emotional day. It's been a roller coaster. It's still all such a surprise."

Although the air had been dense with trade rumors for months, hardly anyone believed they would come true, not even Abbott. "I never thought they'd trade me," he went on, sadly. "I suppose I was naive." But, to his credit, Abbott did get off a well-placed parting shot. "I'm excited to play for a club that wants to win," he declared, thumbing his nose at his tightfisted, short-sighted former bosses.

Abbott could see that the situation on the Angels was not likely to improve—quite the contrary. "When Bryan Harvey left," he noted shortly after his trade, "I stood back and said, 'Where are things going?' It was hurtful to see that kind of person—with that kind of ability—go. At some point, you look around and remember all the people who were here and say, 'What happened to all my friends?' . . . To a man, the people who were the nucleus of the club are gone." Even pitching coach Marcel Lachemann had left to assume those duties with the new Florida Marlins.

On the other hand, the Yankees looked like a team on the way up. Having finished in a disappointing tie for fourth place in 1992, the club made a number of valuable additions for 1993. Besides Abbott, the Yankees also traded for outfielder Paul O'Neill and signed three free agents, third baseman Wade Boggs, left-handed pitcher Jimmy Key, and shortstop Spike Owen. And of course, they already had one of the game's finest players in veteran first baseman Don Mattingly.

The New York Yankees possess one of the grandest histories of any baseball club. Yankee immortals like Ruth, Gehrig, and DiMaggio practically defined the game of baseball for millions. Then there are those latter-day heroes, known by their unforgettable first names—Yogi, Mickey, Reggie, Catfish. Abbott was about to become a part of that heritage, and it thrilled him. "The pinstripes, the tradition of Yankee Stadium, playing with Don Mattingly . . . ," he remarked with the awe of a genuine fan. "I'm excited about those things. I'm not ruling out playing for the Yankees for a long time."

But playing baseball in New York City is a daunting

prospect, and not every player has withstood the pressure. Intense and exhilarating, this great city also can be quite intimidating, especially for a newcomer who has lived in laid-back southern California for four years. Still, Abbott believed he could handle the culture shock. "Hey, I'm a Michigan boy," he reasoned. "Coming to California was a culture shock."

While many New York athletes live in the suburbs, Abbott and his wife, Dana ("a Californian through and through," he noted), decided to take an apartment in Manhattan, nine minutes from Yankee Stadium by cab. That way, they could enjoy New York's vast cultural resources. "We want to experience the city," Abbott announced. "Take in the plays, the museums. We couldn't do that as easily if we lived in New Jersey or Connecticut.

"The way we look at it," he continued, "life is experiences. This will be our New York experience." Seeing a new player—especially one who arrived via a trade that was not his doing—so ready to embrace his new home, refusing to prejudge the city and its people, impressed many New Yorkers.

All winter long, the New York fans kept hearing how hard it was to attract top sports figures to the city. The football Giants had two candidates turn down the head-coaching job simply because neither of them wanted to work in New York— and the Giants actually play their games across the Hudson River in New Jersey! The Yankees courted blue-chip free agents like pitchers Greg Maddux, David Cone, and Doug Drabek, but they all opted to sign with other teams, even though they could have made as much money, or more, playing in New York.

General manager Gene Michael has said that many free agents worry about what he calls "the media crunch," the voracious and influential New York sports writers. "The free agents who can be scared will be scared by the New York media," Michael has claimed. "If they have a legitimate choice between us and another team, then we're not going to be No. 1."

In New York, the press is highly competitive, particularly its notorious tabloids. Sensational headlines attract attention, stimulate curiosity, and sell papers, especially when the story concerns a local sports hero. For many newspaper buyers in this city of sports fanatics, the back-page headline—the *sports* headline—is the first thing they look at when they pick up their daily paper at the newsstand or candy store. New York sports writers know the value of controversy and seek it out. And where there is no controversy, they will do their best to create some, sometimes at the expense of the facts.

So this was the infamous "snake pit" into which Abbott had been plunged. How would he handle it? Right from spring training, Abbott continued to do what he had done in California for the last four years. He didn't hide from the New York writers or get surly with them or try to con them. Instead, he treated the press with cooperation and courtesy. "How many players summon reporters to their lockers to begin scheduled interviews earlier than expected?" wondered an impressed Jack Curry in the *New York Times*.

Then there are the New York sports fans, loyal and tough, often irrational, but as knowledgeable as any fans anywhere. They may knock a player when he is in a slump, but they are quick to forgive and forget when he blasts a game-winning homer or pitches their team to a crucial victory. Many fine players never learn to cope with this volatile atmosphere and wilt under the pressure.

Others agree with Reggie Jackson, who insisted, "New York did bring out the best in me." His five turbulent seasons with the Yankees were a nonstop roller-coaster ride, and if he didn't always enjoy it, Mr. October never let it get the better of

him on the field. "It was fun to play in New York," Jackson recalled. "It was fun to strike out twice and get booed and then hit
a homer the next time up and turn it all around. It was really
fun."

But would Abbott think it was fun? Yankees manager
Buck Showalter realized that his new pitcher had heard all sorts
of stories about New York, so he called Abbott shortly after the
trade. "You'll like the fans," Showalter assured him. "They stay
for the whole game and hang on every pitch, and they know
baseball. They'll cheer for you when you do well and boo when
you don't. But there's an excitement at Yankee Stadium that is
different from Anaheim."

In early February, Abbott traveled to New York, met
some of his new teammates for the first time—although he admitted, "I didn't have the guts to go up and speak to Don Mattingly"—and signed autographs at a baseball-card show. He enjoyed his initial experience with the New York fans, finding
them to be "great and gracious. Of course," he added cautiously,
"I haven't lost a single game yet."

Don Mattingly felt that Abbott had little to worry
about. Any athlete who could triumph over a physical disability
like his, the Yankees captain believed, must possess the kind of
character needed to survive in New York. "Everybody talks
about New York and the fans," Mattingly said early in the season, "but overcoming what he has, and growing up with the cir-
cumstances he did, I think he's better equipped to handle it than
a lot of guys."

But most of all, Abbott would have to handle the Yankees' number-one fan, principal owner George Steinbrenner III.
A witty and intelligent man but an irascible and overbearing
boss, Steinbrenner has attacked players in the press, vilified the
team's stars, capriciously fired and rehired managers, and even
criticized the fans. "George is just like New York," former Yan-

kees relief pitcher Rich "Goose" Gossage has observed. "He can be the nicest guy in the world or 'Bad George.' Dealing with him, and New York, is a true love-hate relationship."

Since July 30, 1990, however, "the Boss" had been frozen in a state of baseball limbo. Because of his dealings with a known gambler, whom he allegedly hired to smear the reputation of former Yankees star Dave Winfield, Steinbrenner was forced by then–Commissioner of Baseball Fay Vincent to resign as the team's managing general partner. Vincent also slapped Steinbrenner with a "lifetime suspension," which barred him from taking any part in the day-to-day running of the team. But after two years and 193 days the ban was lifted, and on March 1, 1993, Steinbrenner would be allowed to resume control of his Yankees.

Asked whether he could get along with his new boss, Abbott responded with his usual discretion. "I have no problem with anything I've ever heard about George Steinbrenner," he insisted. "I mean, it sounds like he wants to have a winner in the worst way. I love that." What else could he say? Certainly there was no point in starting this relationship on the wrong foot. Nevertheless, longtime Steinbrenner watchers couldn't help thinking that Abbott seemed a bit naive. In time, his tactful remarks might fall under the heading "Famous Last Words."

In early January, the Yankees' ownership—sans Steinbrenner, who was still under suspension—met to discuss whether to offer Abbott a multiyear contract. The Yankees had a history of avoiding salary arbitration and had not been engaged in such a hearing since 1988. More than that, Abbott would become eligible for free agency after the 1994 season, his sixth in the major leagues. Having given up three strong prospects for him, it would not look good for the Yankees to lose Abbott after just two years.

"We're interested in signing him if the numbers are

right," announced Joseph Malloy, Steinbrenner's son-in-law, who, in the Boss's absence, was serving as the Yankees' managing general partner. "Once he's in pinstripes, I don't think he'll want to be anywhere else," Malloy added, invoking that famous Yankee arrogance.

On that point, at least, Abbott's agent, Scott Boras, agreed. "I think Jim's view about the Yankees is very, very positive," Boras claimed. "I think he is very interested in playing in New York for a while."

Boras had some preliminary discussions with Bill Bergesch, the Yankee's assistant general manager who handles arbitration cases. After these talks, Bergesch told Malloy that Boras's numbers were too high for a multiyear deal. Boras, it seems, had been touting his client as a "franchise player" similar to Seattle Mariners outfielder Ken Griffey, Jr., who had just signed a four-year, $24 million contract.

Not surprisingly, Malloy dismissed the agent's notion. "They're not in the same category," he remarked. "One pitches every fifth day and one plays every day. You get 30 games out of one and 145 out of the other. That comparison is totally off base."

The contract talks stalled, so an arbitration hearing was scheduled for February 12. Abbott and Boras requested $3.5 million for 1993, an 89 percent increase over his 1992 salary. The Yankees offered $2.35 million. After listening to both sides, the arbitrator ruled in favor of the team.

"I hope there isn't any problem," Gene Michael said when the hearing was over. "This process is not easy for either side, but it's there. It's part of baseball. Unfortunately there has to be a loser." As a player in 1974, Michael lost an arbitration case to the Yankees. His salary at the time was $53,000.

But apparently there were some hard feelings. Boras

would not comment on the Yankees' case or his client's reaction. However, an unnamed person familiar with the hearing told the *New York Times*, "The Yankees used a very negative presentation. Jim wasn't pleased about it."

It was a natural response. At the hearing, the player must listen while the team's representatives try to win their case, and save as much money as they can, by disparaging his performance and potential. The player may understand why the club is saying all these things about him, but that doesn't make it hurt any less. "Why did they trade for me if that's what they think?" Abbott was heard wondering out loud afterward.

This was a new and uncomfortable experience for Abbott. He was a star in Little League and high school, an award-winning college athlete, and an Olympic hero. He had been declared a role model for the disabled and an inspiration to everyone else. With the Angels, he lived a charmed life: fan favorite, darling of the press. All those years filled with success and praise left Abbott unprepared for the harsh reality of his first arbitration hearing.

Throughout his entire athletic career, nobody had ever dared to criticize Jim Abbott, except for some anonymous radio listeners. Even Whitey Herzog, who traded him away, never put down his ability. Abbott simply was not used to having his achievements belittled by the people for whom he worked. It upset him at the hearing, and he reacted in a predictably thin-skinned way.

Less than a week later, Abbott reported to the Yankees' spring training camp in Fort Lauderdale, Florida, still smarting from the experience. "It's not easy coming to a new team and having that be your first association," he reflected. "But arbitration's over now. I have to be grown up about it." And the half-a-million-dollar raise should help ease the pain. "It's more money than I ever dreamed of making," he noted.

Of course, Abbott would have made a lot more—an average of $4 million a year for the next four years—had he and Boras accepted the Angels' offer in October. John Smoltz, for example, a comparable but slightly more successful pitcher (and not a Boras client), accepted a similar offer to stay with Atlanta.

Abbott's case was Boras's fourth consecutive salary-arbitration loss (after an initial victory) of the 1992–93 off-season. Perhaps he was hurting his clients by overvaluing them. "I think their price was too high," Gene Michael said after Abbott's hearing. "I think it's that simple. I think Scott Boras made a mistake with that." In any event, Abbott would not second-guess his agent's advice or his decision to reject the Angels' impressive offer.

"While I was comfortable in California, it was just that," he observed, "comfortable. But I was 7–15 last year and it was no fun. You have to look at the direction a little bit and wonder, do I want to be a part of that for four years?" OK, he would be earning less money but playing for a better club. That was one way to put a positive spin on what could turn out to be a bad move financially, especially if, come October, Abbott found himself without a World Series ring—and bonus.

Meanwhile, the Angels' training camp opened in Mesa, Arizona, and Buck Rodgers tried to put the final period on the "Abbott trade" story. "They'll be talking about Jim Abbott all year," the Angels' manager admitted, and he acknowledged that Abbott's old teammates would feel the void. "You can't blame them. Jim Abbott was a popular guy, and he's still one of my favorites.

"I told him," Rodgers continued, " 'We don't want you to go. It's stupid for you. It's stupid for us.' We just couldn't get past the impasse of the agent. I love Jim Abbott, and I really believe he has a chance to play again in Southern California before it's all over."

It was the company line to the last. Despite his words of affection for the pitcher, Rodgers also was distancing himself from this sticky situation. Three times he referred to his ex-player as "Jim Abbott," rather than the more familiar "Jim" or "Abbie," as his predecessor, Doug Rader, used to call the pitcher.

Moreover, Rodgers's remarks seem designed to create the impression that Abbott left the team entirely of his own accord. (Note how he blamed "the impasse of the agent" without also mentioning "the impasse of the owner's wife.") "A lot of people who have been shooting arrows at us for losing him," Dan O'Brien, the Angels' vice-president for baseball operations, complained in the same vein, "really have no justification."

Sure, the contract talks hit an impasse, and maybe Abbott's demands were too high. But salary arbitration was still an available option. And no attempt to shift the blame to Abbott—or attack his agent—can relieve the Angels front office of its responsibility in this matter. They did not "lose" Abbott, they unloaded him.

Now it was up to the Yankees to try and keep him. Abbott's salary hearing was barely over when Gene Michael suggested that, sometime after March 1, the club might offer the pitcher a long-term contract. "You know what March 1 is, don't you?" the Yankees' general manager asked a reporter, referring to the day Steinbrenner would return to the helm. "I told Boras we wanted to save this for George when he comes back."

In early March, Abbott, after discussions with Boras, announced that he hoped to play in New York for a long time and was eager to begin talks on that elusive multiyear deal. "I'm in the right place at the right time," he insisted. "I guess at some point, you have to stop saying, 'What's out there?' and say, 'Hey, it's pretty good here.' "

The Yankees had acquired some quality players and looked like a contender. New York, Abbott noted, "could be the most exciting place to play in the major leagues." Who could ask for anything more? Now, as far as he was concerned, "the ball [is] in their court. . . . We want to be part of this Yankee organization."

However, when asked about possible contract talks with the pitcher, Steinbrenner replied, "I'm not involved in any of that yet." And two weeks after Abbott's announcement, the club still had not begun negotiations with him.

On the field, Abbott was enjoying the best spring training of his career. He did not allow a single earned run in 21 innings and, on one occasion, provided his new teammates with some Grapefruit League entertainment. In the third inning of an exhibition game against Montreal, Abbott came up to hit against Expos pitcher Chris Nabholz. Using a bat he borrowed from infielder Dave Silvestri, an old teammate from the 1988 Olympics, Abbott took a called strike on a fastball, fouled off two pitches, and took the next one for a ball.

Like most pitchers, Abbott loves to talk about his supposed hitting prowess. (He *almost* hit one out that day in batting practice.) Nonetheless, he waved at a curveball for strike three, while his teammates laughed.

"I hit over .400 in high school . . . but I never saw a curve like that," Abbott insisted. "A lot of guys were saying it was the best curve they've ever seen," he claimed, as if his Yankees teammates never stood in against Bert Blyleven, Roger Clemens, or Nolan Ryan. But a two-strike curveball *to a pitcher?* In an *exhibition game?* What was Nabholz thinking? "I guess he was afraid of my power," Abbott remarked, with a straight face.

For the first time in years, the much-improved Yankees had reason to look forward to Opening Day, and Abbott was glad to be a part of it. "Baseball is fun again," he declared near the end of spring training. "When you are on a team where you have no chance of winning the division, it becomes silent. . . . In here, there's that optimism that makes you get through the day. It's not work. It's fun." He was slated to pitch the second game of the season in Cleveland and then the Yankees' home opener against Kansas City.

Abbott lost that first start, 4–2, but bounced back for his Yankee Stadium debut. As he walked in from the bullpen to start the first inning, the crowd of 56,704 gave Abbott a standing ovation. He thanked them by pitching a 4–1 complete-game victory, giving up eight hits, all singles, and no walks, and striking out four. "That was one of the real highlights of my career," he recalled. "It ranks up there with anything I've ever done, including winning the Olympics."

For whatever reason, Abbott, in his first five major-league seasons, always seemed to get off to a slow start. After four years with the Angels, his record for the month of April was 2–10. Abbott began 1993 with a pair of good starts and a 1–1 record but then struggled through two consecutive disappointing outings. He yielded eight hits and six earned runs in five and two-thirds innings in a 9–0 defeat to the Texas Rangers. Then, Abbott suffered a 6–3 loss to the Seattle Mariners, giving up nine hits and six runs (three earned) in six and two-thirds innings.

On April 27, the Yankees opened a two-game series in California against the Angels. Abbott drove to Anaheim Stadium from his house in Newport Beach, parked his car in the same spot he used for the previous four seasons, walked through the front doors, nodded to the security guard, took the elevator downstairs, and entered the clubhouse—the *visitors'* clubhouse. It was an odd experience, but, he mused, "it wasn't as hard as I thought it would be." He was scheduled to pitch the second game, facing Mark Langston, his best friend and one of the top left-handers in the league. "There are a few other draws I'd rather have," Abbott lamented.

Abbott tried to approach the assignment with big-league professionalism and nonchalance, but the thrill was real and impossible to hide. "It's going to be exciting to pitch in Anaheim again," he acknowledged. "The fans were great to me, but it's one game, and I don't want to make more of it than it is or I won't be able to do my job. I really want to get it behind me and go on."

The crowd of 33,070 gave their old friend a standing ovation as he walked from the visitors' bullpen to the mound. Abbott tried to stay calm, but, he later admitted, his insides were churning as if this were the seventh game of the World Series. "It was a nice feeling," he said, "because I didn't know what to expect. . . . I'm a Yankee now. And you know how everyone hates the Yankees."

He pitched well, certainly well enough to win. Through the first eight innings Abbott gave up just two runs on four hits and one walk. Meanwhile, Langston was simply brilliant. The Angels starter had a no-hitter through the first seven innings. After nine innings, he had yielded two runs on three hits and a walk, striking out 13.

Abbott took the mound in the bottom of the ninth with the score tied, 2–2. Suddenly the Angels' first hitter, rookie outfielder Tim Salmon, ended the pitchers' duel with a home run to left field. Abbott was so stunned that, at first, he didn't realize what had happened. He actually stuck out his glove, waiting for the home-plate umpire to toss him another ball. But when he saw his teammates leaving the field, it finally hit him: the game was over, and he had lost.

Abbott circled the mound twice, walked into the dugout, and flung his glove in disappointment. He sat down on the bench, too numb to move, as the Angels rushed onto the field to celebrate Salmon's game-winning shot. The first player to greet the hitter as he crossed the plate was Mark Langston, who, in the excitement of the moment, seemed to forget that his best friend had been the victim of Salmon's heroics.

"I really feel bad for Jim," Langston said once the scene calmed down, "because it was just an emotional game. I just wish we had hit that homer off someone else, then everything would have been perfect. But it's a business, and you've got to put those feelings away when you walk onto the field."

In the visitors' locker room, Abbott contended with the inevitable postgame questions. "It's going to take a long time for me to get over this," he told the reporters. "The fans were great tonight, and I'll have a lot of good memories, but obviously the home run will be the lingering memory." When the final interview was over, Abbott walked into the trainer's room and screamed, letting out his frustration.

With the season underway, Abbott felt it would be best to hold off on contract talks with the Yankees and focus solely on baseball. In a way, the issue was academic. Steinbrenner had said that signing Abbott to a long-term deal was a priority, but the club still had not made him a concrete offer. Now, a month into the schedule, Abbott vowed that he would neither be distracted by negotiations nor worry about the absence of them.

"There were never any negotiations in spring training and there won't be during the season," he insisted. "I went through enough of that last year. Contract talks are for the off-season. I will concentrate on helping the Yankees have a winning season."

Throughout the early part of 1993, Abbott was hampered by his old nemesis, poor offensive support. In his first six starts, the Yankees scored an average of just 2.17 runs, which, as any big-league pitcher knows, is the shortest route to a 1–5 record. But Abbott also was pitching inconsistently and had problems protecting leads.

In an early May outing against the Tigers, for instance, the Yankees spotted him to a 6–0, first-inning lead. This is the kind of game a pitcher should—indeed, must—win, but somehow Abbott let it slip away. He left the game in the fourth with the bases loaded and no outs, and by the time the inning was over, the score was tied, 7–7. New York went on to win, 10–8, in 11 innings, and Abbott escaped with a no decision.

Still, there were flashes of brilliance. Later that month, he held the Chicago White Sox hitless for seven and one-third innings. But with one out in the eighth, Bo Jackson singled to break up Abbott's no-hit bid. When Jackson reached first base, he gave Abbott a military-style salute. "That guy's a class act," Jackson said of his opponent, who went on to win the game, 8–2.

Jackson had made a remarkable comeback from hip-replacement surgery, and if anybody understood what that meant, Jim Abbott did. "I think the whole world is a Bo Jackson fan," the pitcher declared. "What he has done is an inspiration to a lot of people with physical problems. I always respected him as an athlete, but I respect him all the more as a person. Testimonials aside," Abbott made sure to add, "I still wanted to get him out."

On June 9, in the first inning of a game against Kansas

City, Abbott tore the skin on his thumb. It quickly developed into a blister that made it hard for him to throw his breaking pitch. The thumb worsened, and Abbott had to leave the game after five innings, having allowed six runs on eight hits and four walks.

Seven days later, after he missed a start, the Yankees placed Abbott on the 15-day disabled list, retroactive to June 10. At that point in the season, his record stood at 4–7 with a 4.66 ERA. In 87 innings, Abbott had struck out 40 and allowed 92 hits and 27 walks, mediocre numbers that belied the ability he had shown in past years.

Abbott was activated from the disabled list on June 25. With his thumb problem alleviated, he again was able to mix his pitches effectively, especially against right-handed hitters, and suddenly he got hot. From the last week of June through the end of July, Abbott went 4–1 with an ERA of 2.98, and he had only one poor outing in seven starts. Overall, his record improved to 8–8, and he reduced his ERA to 4.06.

But as July turned into August, Abbott ran into a string of hard luck and bad outings. In his three August losses, the Yankees scored a total of just four runs (4–0, 4–2, 4–2). A 4–1 complete-game win over the Orioles on August 12 was Abbott's only victory of the month.

He also suffered through two horrendous no decisions in August, including a brutal performance in Cleveland at the end of the month. Abbott was knocked out after three and one-third innings, down 7–1—his Bill James game score was a miserable 11—but the Yankees rallied and won, 14–8. Uncharacteristically, Abbott would not speak to reporters after the game.

Meanwhile, the Yankees had jumped into the thick of the pennant race. On July 30 they moved into a first-place tie with the Toronto Blue Jays, and hovered around the top of the

American League East throughout August. At the end of the month, the team acquired reliever Lee Smith, the all-time save leader, to bolster its bullpen for the September stretch drive.

On September 4, it looked as if the "real Jim Abbott" had arrived at last, when he pitched his no-hitter against Cleveland. "It has been a pretty tough season for me," Abbott commented, "but I'm not thinking about that now. I hope this will be a big lift for us. Hopefully we can parlay it into a winning streak."

Unfortunately, Abbott's next start, in Kansas City, embodied the Yankees' September story. He pitched adequately for seven innings but was down, 4–1. The Yankees mounted a four-run comeback in the top of the eighth, however, and Abbott left the game leading, 5–4. The New York bullpen proceeded to blow the lead in the bottom of the inning, and the Yankees went on to lose, 6–5, a no decision for Abbott.

Even since his reinstatement as the Yankees' managing general partner six and a half months earlier, George Steinbrenner had been unusually silent about his team's performance. But now the pennant race was on, his Yankees were stumbling, and the Boss finally erupted.

On September 13, Steinbrenner traveled to Milwaukee, where his team was playing, and held a 25-minute meeting with manager Showalter and the coaching staff. Afterward he spoke to the press. "The guys who haven't done the job know who they are," he told the reporters. To make sure that *everyone* knew who they were, Steinbrenner singled out certain players. One of them was Jim Abbott.

"If we made one calculation that was wrong this year," Steinbrenner spouted, "it's that we had a great pitching staff. . . . We had two guys [Melido Perez and Abbott] who were in the top six in ERA last year.

"If we had gotten the pitching we thought we had, we might have been two games ahead, instead of two games [actually, one and a half games] behind. Let's see if they have enough courage to pick up the slack."

Those were some strong words. They also were ill-timed, ridiculous, and degrading. First of all, with 18 games left to play, it was not as if the Yankees were in imminent danger of falling out of the race. "I don't understand the timing of it or the reason for it," wondered infielder Mike Gallego. "We're one and a half games out. Am I wrong?"

Even stranger was Steinbrenner's remark about courage. "If a player doesn't have courage," shot back *New York Times* sports columnist Dave Anderson, "he wouldn't be in the big leagues." But for Steinbrenner to question the courage of Jim Abbott, of all people, was inconceivably bizarre. To have done so in as public a manner as this was inexcusably vicious.

"If he singled me out as being disappointing this year," Abbott said, reacting to Steinbrenner's statements, "nobody likes to hear that. He owns the team and is entitled to his opinion and judgment." Abbott is the kind of athlete who responds well to pressure on the field, but not to criticism off it, and the Steinbrenner attack was only part of the problem. It looked like he was starting to feel the strain of life in the big city.

"New York is New York," he told the *New York Times*'s Jack Curry in early September. "It seems like it magnifies everything by five or ten times. . . . When you win, it's the greatest thing. When you lose, it's harsh."

With the Angels, Abbott enjoyed a cozy relationship with a compliant, forgiving press corps. He wasn't used to questions like, "Do you think you are earning your salary?" or the bold, blunt back-page headlines that are the staples of New York sports journalism. "I'm the kind of person who worries about what people think," he continued. "If something is written that is harsh or that I don't appreciate, I take it hard."

Abbott reproached the New York press for the way it was evaluating his 1993 performance. "It's not a great season, but it's not a terrible season," he insisted. "Wins and losses aren't always in a pitcher's control. You can give up one unearned run in nine innings and still lose." True enough, but that was not the kind of year Abbott was having. He had been inconsistent all season long, so Steinbrenner's verbal assault contained, perhaps, a kernel of truth: if the Yankees were to remain in contention, Abbott would have to pitch better down the stretch.

Abbott's next start, two days after Steinbrenner's attack, was a complete disaster. He opened the game by giving up a leadoff double followed by three straight walks, but somehow got out of the inning with only one run scored against him. In the second, however, the Brewers attacked Abbott for four runs, and he was knocked out of the game after just one and two-thirds innings.

It was his shortest outing of the season—with a poor game score of 21—and the second shortest of his career. None of the other New York pitchers that day were any better, and the Yankees lost, 15–5. Did the Boss's criticism affect his performance? "No, I didn't think about it," Abbott claimed, unconvincingly.

The Yankees limped through the final two weeks of the season and wound up in second place with an 88–74 record, seven games behind Toronto. For much of the second half, the team stayed near the top of the division, but an 11–15 September proved to be their undoing. The starting rotation was just 6–12 with a 4.65 ERA for the month, and Lee Smith earned only three saves. Apparently, Steinbrenner's criticism did little to inspire his players. The Yankees played .500 ball (9–9) after the Boss's Milwaukee visit.

Abbott had opened September with the game of his career, but he pitched erratically for the remainder of the season. After the no-hitter, he won one and lost three with a 6.07 ERA, and in 29⅔ innings he gave up 40 hits and 11 walks, striking out only 10. On the year, Abbott was 11–14 with an ERA of 4.37. In 214 innings he struck out 95, a significant drop from 1992, when he struck out 130 in 211 innings. He certainly did not look like a $4 million pitcher.

It would be unfair to hang the Yankee's 1993 near miss on any one or two players. Losing, like winning, is a team effort. Still, great things were expected of Abbott when he came to New York, and he failed to deliver more than a small portion of them. Likewise, in 1992 right-hander Melido Perez was sixth in the American League with a 2.87 ERA. In 1993, Perez's ERA nearly doubled (5.19), he won six and lost 14, and he was unable to pitch after September 3 because of a sore right shoulder.

"If Melido Perez and Jim Abbott had combined for 25 victories, a modest goal in April, the American League East may have had a different complexion," Jack Curry wrote after the season ended. The math could not be simpler: together Abbott and Perez won just 17 and the Yankees came in second by seven games. Eight more wins from them could have put the team over the top. Steinbrenner tried to make that point when he singled out the two pitchers in mid-September. He wasn't wrong in what he said, only in the timing and manner in which he said it.

As the 1993 schedule wound down, speculation began anew that Abbott would file for free agency after the 1994 season. A return to the Angels seemed a likely scenario. In September, California signed left-hander Joe Magrane, a sore-armed St. Louis Cardinals castoff, to a three-year contract potentially worth $9.3 million. A healthy-armed Jim Abbott, Scott Boras figured, had to be worth a good deal more than that.

"We're talking about a guy who was released a month ago," Abbott's agent observed, "and look what he got. It just shows you how much of a pitching shortage there is. If Jim wants to come back [to the Angels], and that's what makes him happy, I'd be all for it."

Maybe Boras was putting the Yankees on notice. No-hitter or not, the last month of the 1993 season had left a bad taste in his client's mouth, but a multiyear deal could make it go away. After his struggling performance, however, Abbott not only would have to convince the front office that he deserved a lucrative, long-term contract. It seemed like he would have to convince himself, as well.

8

⌒○ The Long,
Short Season

"**O**nce I got away from the [1993] season," Jim Abbott told then–*New York Daily News* columnist Mike Lupica when spring training opened in mid-February, "people mostly wanted to talk about the no-hitter. They'd actually come up to me and say, 'Great season.' "

But 1993 was not a great season for Abbott, not even a good one. He knew that better than anyone, and he took it hard. "There were times during the season when I had to make a heavy withdrawal on the confidence I had built up over the years," he admitted to Lupica. "I'm not saying I was miserable all the time. . . . But I definitely had to dip into that reservoir of belief in myself."

So Abbott spent what he called a "recuperative" winter. After the season ended, he and Dana enjoyed a month in north-

ern Michigan, relaxing in their cabin by Lake Michigan. Relax-
ation was exactly what Abbott needed. He decided to refine his
attitude and learn not to torture himself whenever he made a
mistake on the mound. "I used to wear that as a badge of courage," he observed. "You should be hard on yourself. That's what
got you here. That's what I thought. I understand now that
maybe it can be a negative."

Perhaps out of the adversity of 1993 would come maturity. Abbott had heard it before, that he didn't need to be so
intense all the time, but now, at the age of 26, as a five-year
major-league veteran, the lesson finally seemed to be sinking in.
All season long he watched fellow Yankees starter Jimmy Key
and resolved to be more like the unflappable lefty. Of course,
with an 18-6 record, 4.02 strikeout-to-walk ratio, and a 3.00
ERA in 1993, Key had few occasions to be hard on himself.

Abbott claimed that he did not consult a sports psychologist during the off-season. However, he talked with professors
who, as he put it, "deal with the mental side of the game"—in
other words, sports psychologists. He also spent time reading bi-
ographies, hoping to learn how people he admires, such as Abraham Lincoln, handled difficult situations in their lives.

One difficult situation that Abbott hoped to avoid was
another acrimonious salary arbitration hearing. But again, the
Yankees did not come up with a long-term contract. Instead,
they offered him a one-year deal worth $2.65 million, $300,000
more than his 1993 salary. Abbott declined, decided to file for
arbitration, and submitted a salary figure of $2.9 million.

It was hard for Abbott to escape the nagging feeling that
the front office was pinning the near miss of 1993 largely on
him. After all, during the off-season general manager Gene Michael said that if Abbott and Melido Perez "pitched the way we
thought they would, we could have won the whole thing." Ab-

bott resented that notion. "I don't think I personally held the Yankees back," he responded. "I hope the Yankees still have confidence in what I can do."

Shortly before the start of spring training, Abbott and the Yankees managed to avoid arbitration by agreeing to split the difference in their salary figures. He signed a one-year contract that would pay him $2.775 million in 1994. Still, the lack of a multiyear deal bothered him. Did the Yankees' front office expect—maybe even hope—that he would file for free agency and move on once the season was over?

"I'd like to stay here," Abbott repeated in the press for what seemed like the thousandth time. "I'm just concerned with going out and playing well. That stuff will take care of itself." The more he said it, the more it sounded like wishful thinking.

One thing Abbott did know was that he and Dana would not be living in Manhattan once the season started. They considered moving to either nearby Westchester County in New York State or northern New Jersey, but they finally settled on the suburban town of Greenwich, Connecticut. This was part of his plan to relax. By leaving the city, Abbott could avoid the barrage of tabloid headlines that blared at him from every city street-corner newsstand and candy store.

As Jon Heyman of *New York Newsday* noted, Abbott reads everything written about him, worries about everything he reads, and worse, believes some of it. He is, in Heyman's view, "by almost all definitions a classic overachiever, [who] occasionally was portrayed in the newspapers as an underachiever last year. It hurt him." A home in the suburbs might serve as a retreat from the pressure of the daily press, but only if Abbott could learn to stop taking the headlines so seriously. Today's tabloids, he needed to remind himself constantly, are tomorrow's fish wrappings.

On the field, it was an optimistically uneventful spring training for Abbott. In his first two starts, he shut out opposing batters for a total of seven innings, which extended his streak of scoreless exhibition-game innings (since 1993) to 28. In his third spring outing, however, the Dodgers cuffed him for 10 runs and 11 hits in four innings. Los Angeles went on to win the slug-fest, 18-10.

The battering, he said afterward, was the result of "no-decision change-ups, where the hitter didn't have any decision to make, they were so far out of the strike zone." Still, he wasn't discouraged. After five years in the majors, Abbott knew how much stock to put in spring training games. "My fastball control has improved," he commented, "I have better extension out in front of my delivery. See, those are the things I look for.

"You know," he continued, "I've seen guys go out and look terrible in spring training, then go out and win their first seven ballgames. This time of year, it's the process over the product."

Abbott rebounded and pitched fairly well for the rest of the exhibition season. Although he yielded four first-inning runs in his next start, also against the Dodgers, he settled down, pitched five shutout innings, and won, 8-4. Abbott held the Red Sox to two runs on seven hits in five and one-third innings in his last spring appearance. In five spring outings, he won two and lost one, and his ERA was a deceptive 6.45. Not counting the first Dodgers game, Abbott was 2-0 with a solid 2.95 ERA.

But off the field, life turned rocky for Abbott. On February 25, in an otherwise pleasant and low-key 20-minute visit with reporters, George Steinbrenner suddenly began blaming Abbott's subpar 1993 performance on his "other activities," that is, his charity work and visits with disabled children. "Jim Abbott's got to give 100 percent of his attention to baseball," Steinbrenner told the stunned journalists. "Jim Abbott is the kind of young man who is going to go out and do other activities. There's only so much you can do, and do your best.

"There are too many demands on his time," the Yankees' owner continued, making matters worse with every sentence. "I'm going to tell Jim Abbott to cut down. . . . He wasn't there last year. He knows that. Everybody knows that."

Steinbrenner's mouth routinely runs out of control, but this was remarkable, even for him. It takes an exceptionally cold character to criticize a man for doing good works. Realizing what he had done, the Boss tried to control the damage. "Put this down," he instructed the reporters, " 'George is not putting pressure on Jim Abbott.' " By then, however, it was too late. The reporters had already composed the leads for their stories.

Here was one time when the often overly sensitive Abbott had a real reason to be angry. When informed of Steinbrenner's statement, he nearly shot back. No one would have blamed him if he did. "I don't like to be told—," Abbott began, but he cut himself off and decided to tone down his response. "If anyone has the impression that I'm not giving the effort I should," he resumed, regaining his composure, "there's a lot of misinformation there."

He insisted that his meetings with disabled kids were "a five- or 10-minute thing." In addition, most of Abbott's charitable activities actually were set up or approved by the team. "If they want me to curtail those things and think I'll be a better player because of it," he conceded, "that's what I'll do."

It's a sad and sickening thought that Abbott should feel

compelled to downplay and justify the many helpful and caring things he does. "Jim Abbott just can't say no," *New York Newsday* reporter Mark Hermann has observed, with deserved admiration. "Not to the Little League Challenger Division program, not to the children's agencies for which he does extensive fundraising, not for any kid who wants to say hello and believes he or she can be inspired by meeting the pitcher who was born without a right hand."

Abbott's inability to say no to kids in need earned him the Freedom Foundation's "Free Spirit Award" for 1993. (Previous winners include Associated Press reporter and Lebanon hostage Terry Anderson, and former Supreme Court justices William Brennan and Thurgood Marshall.) At the awards dinner, held that October at the New York Public Library, Abbott and co-honoree Eunice Kennedy Shriver each received $100,000 to donate to charities of their choice. Abbott presented his check to Amigos de los Niños, a California organization that assists groups that care for children.

In the sports world of today, the "greedy professional athlete" is a pervasive notion, sometimes justifiably so, more often not. Abbott is one strong counterargument to that stereotype. So are many of his teammates. Mike Gallego, who himself overcame testicular cancer, is active in the fight against cancer in children. Wade Boggs raises huge amounts of money each year for multiple sclerosis research and treatment. And Don Mattingly's charity list takes up 10 lines in the Yankees' media guide. Steinbrenner's record, on the other hand, is somewhat less commendable. In the 1970s, he was convicted of making illegal campaign contributions to Richard Nixon.

Nine days later, Steinbrenner met with Abbott to "explain" his comments, and the matter was never again mentioned in public by either party. Still, the season hadn't even started and Abbott already had one less reason to stay with the Yankees after it was over.

Every Opening Day all the musty, old sports-writing clichés are aired out: a "clean slate," a "fresh start," "it's anybody's year," and so on. They may be banal, but that doesn't mean these well-worn sentiments don't apply. For Jim Abbott, preparing to face the 1994 baseball season, they applied all too well.

Yankees fans were frustrated with Abbott's inconsistency in 1993, and they had a right to be. But, as the director told the ingenue in *42nd Street*, "Those people in the audience *want* to like you." It seemed that every time he took the mound that year, Yankees fans were pulling for Abbott, not simply because he pitched for the home team, but also because they liked him.

Abbott did give them a few, precious glimpses of greatness: the strong home opener against the Royals, the nine-inning heartbreaker against the Angels in Anaheim, the near no-hitter against the White Sox, and, of course, the no-hitter in September. But now, the high highs and even lower lows of 1993 were consigned to record books and memories. It was a new season, and Abbott knew what his job was: maintain control over all his pitches, challenge the hitters, protect leads, pitch out of jams, and, most important, string wins together.

The 1994 season brought a change for major-league baseball. The teams in each league were realigned and divided into three, rather than two, divisions. The postseason schedule also was restructured and expanded, incorporating a "wild card" concept borrowed from professional football. Not only would the three divisional champions in each league advance to the first round of the playoffs, but so would the second-place team with the most victories.

Had the new alignment and playoff system been in effect in 1993, the Yankees, with their 88 wins, would have been the American League wild-card team. But with the start of the new season, no one in New York was thinking about second place. Having added lefty starter Terry Mulholland (12-9, 3.25 ERA with the Phillies in 1993), reliever Xavier Hernandez (nine saves, 2.61 ERA in a setup role with Houston), and speedy outfielder Luis Polonia (55 stolen bases, .271 batting average with the Angels) to an already-strong roster, the 1994 Yankees looked ready to battle the world-champion Toronto Blue Jays for the top spot in the American League East.

But a dark specter hung over the start of the 1994 season. On December 31, 1993, the collective bargaining agreement between the cartel of team owners and the Major League Baseball Players Association, the union that represents the players, expired. In January, the owners of less profitable, small-market franchises, like Milwaukee and Seattle, convinced their brethren to accept a new revenue-sharing system. According to this plan, the more profitable, large-market teams would transfer a portion of the income they received from lucrative local-broadcasting deals to the less economically viable clubs.

But the large-market owners wanted something in exchange for this revenue-sharing arrangement. As a condition of the agreement, they insisted that any new contract with the players' union include a salary-cap provision. This would set a monetary ceiling on what major-league teams may spend on their payrolls, in effect limiting the amount that players can be paid.

The owners predicted that 19 of the 28 major-league teams would lose money in 1994. As a consequence, they argued, there needed to be a radical change in the way baseball conducts its business, specifically in how it handles its salary structure. The Players Association wanted the owners to prove their claim and asked that independent auditors be allowed to inspect each team's financial records. The owners, however, refused to open their books. They promised to disclose the specifics of their proposal sometime in June.

Well before Opening Day it was clear that, without proof, the players' union would not accept a salary cap in any form. It was equally clear that the owners were adamant on this issue. If the union did not agree to their scheme, the owners, after the season was over, could declare an impasse in the negotiations and unilaterally impose the cap (and possibly eliminate free agency and salary arbitration, as well). To head off such an action, the players might have to call on the only real weapon at their disposal: a strike against major-league baseball.

So under this ominous cloud, New York started the season by taking two straight from the Texas Rangers. Abbott got his first turn on the mound at home against the Detroit Tigers. A sparse Friday night crowd of only about 20,000 turned out at Yankee Stadium, but those who decided to brave the chilly, early-spring weather were treated to some impressive early-season pitching.

Abbott was sharp and aggressive, jamming right-handed hitters inside with his slider. He shut the Tigers out through seven innings and enjoyed a four-run lead when Buck Showalter decided he had done enough work that night. Abbott already had thrown 99 pitches—68 of them for strikes—and the Yankees manager didn't want to overwork his pitcher so early in the season, especially with the temperature falling into the 40s. Reliever Bob Wickman faltered, but Steve Howe came in to save the 4-0 win.

In seven innings, Abbott allowed just five baserunners (three hits and two walks) and struck out eight, his most ever as a Yankee. Even more important, he was able to keep minor threats from becoming major disasters. The first hitter of the game reached base on an error. In the fourth inning, the Tigers put runners on second and third with two outs. And in the seventh, their leadoff hitter doubled. Each time, Abbott kept his poise and retired the side before any damage could be done.

"I've worked hard on that," he said with pride. "I want my teammates to know if they make a mistake or I make a mistake, it's not going to blow up into a huge inning." It was, in every way, as strong a 1994 debut as the Yankees and their fans could have asked from Abbott. New York had won their first three games of the season, and for the first time in his six-year major-league career, Abbott started with a victory.

For five years, Abbott, try as he might, never really was able to develop an effective change-up to offset his fastball and slider. It was truly a mystery how such a valuable weapon could elude a pitcher with his mechanics, intelligence, and capacity for hard work. But the Yankees' first-base coach, Brian Butterfield, had a theory.

During spring training, Butterfield noticed that, whenever Abbott got ready to deliver a pitch to the plate, he could see the ball from the first-base coaching box. Many pitchers hide the ball in their gloves until just before they begin their windup. However, because of Abbott's glove-hand switch, the pocket of his glove faces away from his body and toward first base, so the ball is visible between pitches. Perhaps, Butterfield surmised, opposing coaches are able to detect Abbott's change-up grip and signal the hitters.

Hoping to prevent this, the Yankees devised a new glove for Abbott, with a three-inch leather flap to hide his grip. He warmed up with it before his second start of the season, in Chicago. The umpiring-crew chief, Don Denkinger, said that it would be all right for Abbott to use the new glove in the game if he chose to do so. "It's up to him whether he wants to use it or not," Showalter announced.

However, Abbott took the mound in the bottom of the first wearing his usual glove. After all, since he had pitched so well in his last start, there seemed to be little reason to make a change. But there was more to it than that. After the game, press reports indicated that Abbott felt "uncomfortable" with the new glove, and it was easy to see why.

All his life, Abbott refused any kind of special attention or treatment simply because he was born with only one hand. Through patience and hard work he learned a way to beat the two-handed guys at their own game. But more than that, here he was, in his sixth major-league season, completely blended in, regarded as just another pitcher, sometimes good, sometimes not so good. Now, his team wanted to undo all that by giving him a piece of special equipment, a baseball prosthesis reminiscent of the hated "hook" that he refused to use when he was five years old.

What Abbott really needed that night was not a new glove, but some bats. The White Sox pitchers shut out the Yankees on five hits. Abbott gave up four runs (one unearned) on eight hits in six and two-thirds innings. Most alarming, the command of the strike zone that he showed last time out seemed to evaporate, as Abbott yielded four walks and struck out only three. It was a disappointing effort all around, and Abbott was stuck with his first loss of the season, 5-0.

In Abbott's next start, at home against the Seattle Mariners, he fell behind 4-0 after the second inning, and the Yankees had good reason to worry. When Abbott's slider breaks down and in on a right-handed batter's fists, as it did against the

Tigers earlier in the month, it is virtually unhittable. When that same pitch hangs up in the strike zone, as it did on this night, it's batting practice.

Jay Buhner led off the third inning for the Mariners. An ex-Yankee, Buhner was traded to Seattle in July 1988, and he has punished his former team ever since. Going into this game, the lifetime .253 hitter was batting .312 against New York with 11 home runs—nine of them in Yankee Stadium—and 35 RBIs in 154 at bats. To make matters worse, Buhner came into the game with a lifetime .410 average against Abbott, and he already had an RBI single in the top of the first.

Sure enough, Abbott served up one of those dangerous hanging sliders, and Buhner launched a 430-foot moon shot high and deep over the left-field wall. He came up again in the fifth, this time with a runner on first. Abbott got Buhner in a 0-2 hole, with two good sliders down and in. His third slider, however, stayed up in the strike zone and this time Buhner drove another home run even deeper into the left-field seats, for his third and fourth RBIs of the game.

Abbott was through after five innings, down 7-0, and since all the Yankees offense could muster was a single run in the ninth, he was charged with the 7-1 loss. It was a frustrating outing. Early in the game Abbott had trouble getting his curve and change-up over the plate, so he had to rely on his fastball and slider. On the whole, his control was not that bad—he didn't walk any batters and got nearly two-thirds of his pitches in for strikes. The problem was that they were hittable strikes, because the slider didn't slide and the fastball was not fast enough.

The Mariners claimed that they clocked Abbott's fastball at only 82 miles per hour on their radar gun. The Yankees disputed the figure, but, as one of the most secretive organizations in sports, they would not disclose their readings. Nevertheless, the Mariners' report supported the widespread belief throughout the American League that Abbott had lost significant speed on his fastball, which never was all that overpowering in the first place.

Before Abbott's next start, against the Oakland Athletics in Yankee Stadium, an unnamed Yankees official asked the umpires whether Abbott could use the special glove in the game if New York got a lead. The crew chief, Jim Evans, replied that, if Abbott wanted to use the glove, it would have to be for the entire game. When he took the mound for the first inning, Abbott had his regular glove with him.

It was a moot point. Everything that Abbott could not do five days earlier against the Mariners, he did against the Athletics. He worked both sides of the plate and was able to mix his pitches. His slider broke, his fastball moved, and the Oakland hitters were confounded. Abbott held the Athletics hitless for seven and one-third innings, and he left the game after the eighth with a 6-1 lead, having struck out six and allowing just three hits.

Reliever Jeff Reardon yielded a solo homer in the ninth. Still, Abbott came away with his second victory of the young season, 6-2, the streaking Yankees got their seventh win in eight games, and the matter of the special glove was put to rest for good.

Abbott faced the Athletics again in Oakland five days later, but a shaky first inning told an ominous tale. Two deep fly-ball outs—one caught at the right-field wall, the other caught *above* the left field wall—and two walks announced that Abbott was either hanging his pitches up in the strike zone or missing it altogether. The Yankees scored six runs in the first two innings, and it looked like Abbott might need all of them, and more, before the night was over.

For five innings, he teetered on the edge of disaster. He wasn't beating the Athletics, they were beating themselves. Twice Oakland left the bases loaded, and two more times they left two runners on. Still, they managed to score four runs on eight hits and eight walks, while the struggling Abbott notched only a single strikeout. He left the game after the fifth, leading 6-4.

The Yankees scored more runs, got good relief pitching from Xavier Hernandez, and, thanks in large part to Luis Polonia's hitting (three doubles, two runs scored, and three runs batted in), came out on top, 10-6. Abbott pitched just badly enough to win—his game score was 28, well below average, especially in a winning effort. The cheap victory gave him a 3-2 record for the month of April. For the first time in his career, Abbott had won more than one game in the opening month of the season, and his ERA was a solid 3.41.

Throughout the first month of the season, Yankees pitching coach Billy Connors kept telling Abbott not to throw to the same spot all the time, namely, inside to right-handed batters. Sooner or later, Connors warned, the hitters will adjust their swing and begin to make good contact, which is exactly what happened in Abbott's ugly outing in Oakland. In his next start, against the Angels in Anaheim, Abbott took Connors's advice and it paid off. Three of his four strikeouts were on pitches away.

Abbott pitched fairly well—he gave up only three hits and two unearned runs in six innings and left the game leading 5-2—but he still seemed to be fighting his control, walking four batters and falling behind on others. Showalter turned the game over to Jeff Reardon, who came into the season second on the all-time save list with 365 but now was struggling to hang on to his career. Reardon allowed three runs on four hits and lasted just one-third of an inning. Two days later, he was waived from the Yankees' roster.

Abbott's bid for a win had been blown, and the game, tied 5-5, went into extra innings. Both teams scored in the tenth. The Yankees nearly broke the deadlock in the top of the thirteenth inning, but center fielder Chad Curtis heaved a perfect throw to nail Don Mattingly at the plate. California scored in the bottom of the inning, ending the four-hour-26-minute marathon. Five days earlier, Abbott won a game he should have lost. This time, in a game he should have won, he came up empty.

Back in New York, Abbott faced Cleveland and the kid from Washington Heights, Manny Ramirez. Ramirez, who would turn 22 on May 30, batted his way onto the Cleveland roster during spring training, but after a strong start he had gone hitless in his last 17 at bats. Playing at home, with friends and family members stationed in the left-field seats, Ramirez was ready to get back on track. His sacrifice fly in the second inning tied the game, 1-1, and "Section Ramirez" cheered as if he had hit a grand-slam home run.

New York retook the lead, 4-1, in the bottom of the fourth. Ramirez broke out of his slump in the fifth with a long solo home run into the left-field stands. With the score still 4-2, he led off the seventh with a double down the left-field foul line that caromed off the top of the wall, missing a second home run by inches and thrilling his rooting section. But in baseball, it is awfully easy to go from hero to goat.

The next hitter, Alvaro Espinoza, laid down an apparent sacrifice bunt. Inexplicably, Ramirez, perhaps thinking about the home run he had just missed, did not advance to third base. Then Tony Peña grounded to shortstop, and Ramirez, trying to make up for his previous mistake, committed another. Violating a cardinal rule of baserunning, he tried to advance to third on a ground ball hit in front of him and was thrown out easily. If Ramirez had gone to third on Espinoza's bunt, he might have scored on Peña's grounder, and Cleveland would have been down by only one run.

With two out and none on in the eighth, Albert Belle blasted a hanging Abbott slider into the Cleveland bullpen, 420 feet away in left center, to make the score 4-3. Eddie Murray doubled to left and, with the tying run in scoring position, Showalter decided to call on his bullpen. This time it came through for Abbott, as Bob Wickman put out the fire and Xavier Hernandez came on in the ninth to save the win.

Except for the two home runs, Abbott had shown real savvy on the mound, moving the ball around the plate and retiring hitters with "heat outside," fastballs up and away. He struck out seven and walked only two, one of his strongest control performances so far. Best of all, the victory moved the Yankees into sole possession of first place, and gave them a record of 20-10, New York's best 30-game start since 1953.

In his next outing, Abbott pitched six innings against the struggling Milwaukee Brewers and was in trouble during every one. He allowed a total of 10 base runners (five hits and five walks), and two more Brewers reached base because of errors by shortstop Mike Gallego. But losing teams lose because they can't convert runners into runs. Milwaukee managed to score only twice, once on an Abbott balk.

Abbott left the game down 2-1, with New York's eight-game winning streak in jeopardy. But the Yankees were making a habit of late-game heroics, having pulled out their last two victories in extra innings. Once again, they came through in the clutch, rallying in the top of the ninth to score five runs. The streak was extended and Abbott was off the hook.

Abbott recovered from his erratic outing in Milwaukee and notched his fifth win of the season against the Baltimore Orioles, 5-1. In seven innings of work, he allowed a few too many base runners (11) and struck out only one batter. Nevertheless, by keeping the ball down in the strike zone and changing speeds, Abbott managed to stop the bleeding with timely ground-ball outs, including two double plays.

But a potentially bigger story was unfolding 3,000 miles away. Three days earlier, the California Angels had fired their manager, Buck Rodgers, and replaced him with Abbott's friend and former pitching coach, Marcel Lachemann. "I'm thrilled for Lach," Abbott said when he heard the news. "He's an extremely loyal and hard-working man. . . . If you struggle, he'll be in your corner." He was speaking from experience, recalling how, when he hit a rough spot early in the 1991 season, Lachemann stood behind him and fought to keep Abbott from being sent to the minors.

With free agency approaching and Abbott's long-term status with the Yankees still unresolved, a return to the Angels was now an increasingly appealing, and likely, option for 1995. In addition to Lachemann's hiring, pitcher Mark Langston, Abbott's closest friend on the Angels, had signed a contract extension through 1997. Another friend, Tim Mead, Abbott's personal public-relations liaison and gatekeeper during his four years with the club, recently was promoted to the position of assistant general manager.

Abbott continued to insist that he enjoyed playing for a strong Yankees club and that he would make no decisions about next season until the end of this one. Still, these developments in California raised the stakes considerably for Abbott, as well as for the Yankees front office.

Toward the end of May, the Toronto Blue Jays arrived in New York for a two-game series against the Yankees. Before the first game, Joe Carter, the Blue Jays' right fielder and cleanup hitter, mused about what he calls the "George Factor." "It's definitely tough playing in New York," he remarked. "It makes it tougher, playing for George. You know he's going to be looking down upon you." Thus, the George Factor, Carter figured, is "good for two or three [Yankees] losses down the road."

Toronto center fielder Devon White agreed, recalling how Steinbrenner questioned his team's character and courage in the midst of last September's pennant race. "He tends to shake up a lot of people, and they go into a panic," White observed. "It seems that's what happened last year and they went downhill." As the Yankees faltered, the Blue Jays went on to win the division, the American League pennant, and the World Series.

But except for Steinbrenner's graceless spring-training criticism of Abbott's charity work, the George Factor was a non-factor so far in 1994, to their opponents' chagrin. The Yankees beat Toronto, 6-1, in the first game of this short series. In the second one, the Blue Jays had all they could do to handle the Jim Factor and the Wade Factor.

Abbott was masterful, mixing all his pitches—fastball, slider, curve, and change-up—and delivering them with location and movement. He had to sit through a 90-minute rain delay in the middle of the fourth inning but returned to the mound as sharp and as loose as when he left it. Abbott stayed on to pitch the remaining five innings for his first complete game of the season, allowing two runs—both scored by White and driven in by Carter—on just six hits and two walks.

Then there was Wade Boggs. Suffering from bruised and sore ribs, Boggs had his body tightly wrapped before the game so that he could play with as little pain as possible. Ever the student of hitting, he believed that the bandage actually added punch to his already-superb stroke. "The rib wrap is limiting my swing to be short and compact," Boggs explained. "I'm waiting to explode at the last second."

And explode he did. The Yankees third baseman went four for five that night, including two home runs—a two-run blast and a solo shot. (Boggs, who also hit a rib-wrap dinger the night before, had only two home runs in all of 1993.) Danny Tartabull also contributed a solo homer to Abbott's 5-2 victory.

For Abbott, the season seemed to be breezing along. He felt more relaxed and focused on the mound, which, he believed, was the reason for his early-season success. "The basic technique is to reduce the game to one pitch at a time," Abbott explained. "I know that's a cliché, but that is key. It's all about 'this pitch.' I can't do anything about the pitch before or the pitch after until I throw this one.

"I'm in control of myself," he went on. "I've made my [pitch] selection. I have my location. Now I've got to trust it. If all those things are intact, I've got a pretty good chance of making a good pitch." So far, everything looked great for Abbott: his team was in first place, his ERA was down to 2.67, and, with a 6-2 record after 10 starts, he seemed like a good bet to win at least 16—maybe 18—games. George Factor? What George Factor?

But, on closer inspection, these optimistic appearances proved somewhat deceiving. Hall of Famer Lefty Gomez, who pitched for the Yankees in the 1930s, used to say, "I'd rather be lucky than good." In his 7-15 1992 season, Abbott was good but unlucky, the victim of an abysmal offense. Through his first 10 starts in 1994, on the other hand, he was lucky but not really that good.

Abbott's strikeout-to-walk ratio for those 10 games was just 1.14, and he allowed an average of 12.7 baserunners per every nine innings. So far, reliable fielding—especially strong double-play support—had prevented most of those runners from becoming runs, and clutch hitting usually kept the Yankees in the game. Perhaps Abbott really did feel more comfortable on the mound, or perhaps he was living in a fool's paradise. The season was young, and luck has a way of running out. The wisdom of Lefty Gomez notwithstanding, it's best to be both lucky *and* good.

As if on schedule, Abbott hit the skids, dropping his next three starts, a disappointing 7-2 game against the White Sox, a tough 3-1 loss to the Royals, and a mediocre nine-hit, six-run, six-inning performance against the Blue Jays. The danger signs now were clear. He was not getting his breaking pitch in on right-handers, and he was not working the outside of the plate at all. Abbott was throwing almost no off-speed pitches, relying on a fastball that was not very fast.

On June 14, the major-league team owners made their specific salary-cap proposal to the players' union. Along with this scheme to limit how much major leaguers could earn, the owners also proposed to eliminate salary arbitration and to allow free agency after four years of major-league service, instead of the current six. But is any free-agency system really "free" if it restricts how much players may be paid? In mid-July, the union, to no one's surprise, rejected the owners' plan, and a strike seemed likely.

Abbott's next outing, on June 15 in Baltimore, proved that "dee-fense" is important not only in football. At least six times in the game, solid fielding prevented runs and stopped rallies. For instance, in the second inning, with runners on second and third and the score tied, 2-2, Mike Devereaux sent a pop fly into short right-center. Yankees second baseman Pat Kelly made an over-the-shoulder catch to retire the hitter and save at least one run.

In the third, Chris Sabo hit a shot along the third-base line that should have been a double, but Wade Boggs knocked it down, picked it up, and threw Sabo out at first. Rafael Palmeiro drove a high strike into deep left field, but a leaping Paul O'Neill snagged the ball at the top of the wall for out number two. Then Cal Ripken pounded another Abbott hanger into deep center field. This time, Bernie Williams jumped to make the catch above the wall. Instead of a double and two home runs, it was three up, three down, and the score still tied.

Abbott helped his own cause in the fourth inning, turning a comeback groundball into a nifty 1-6-3 double play. And in the fifth, with runners on second and third and one out, Palmeiro hit a fly to center field. Williams made the catch and uncorked a perfect throw to nail the lead runner at the plate, ending the inning. Abbott left the game with a 4-3 lead, but the bullpen crumbled and the Yankees, despite their good play in the field, lost 8-4.

The Baltimore game revealed one of Abbott's biggest problems in 1994. He failed to retire the Orioles' leadoff batter in five of the seven innings he pitched. Through his first 14 starts, leadoff hitters had a .439 on-base percentage against Abbott, the second highest in the American League. In other words, he allowed the first batter of the inning to get on base almost 44 percent of the time. "None out, one (or worse, two) on" is a tailor-made run-scoring situation, and pitchers can't always expect their defense to bail them out.

Abbott labored against Minnesota on June 20—five runs on 12 hits in five and one-third innings—and left on the losing side, 5-2. However, the slumping Yankees, who were 6-12 so far in June, pulled ahead, 7-5, on Daryl Boston's pinch-hit three-run homer in the eighth, and Abbott escaped with another no decision.

Cleveland leadoff hitters went three for six in Abbott's next outing, but he left the game leading, 8-4. New York scored four more times and, with the score now 12-4, the victory seemed in hand. Suddenly, Cleveland mounted a seven-run rally in the bottom of the eighth and the Yankees barely squeaked by, 12-11. Abbott was credited with the win, his first in his last six starts.

Abbott opened the month of July with a good game against Seattle, allowing only two earned runs in eight innings' work. He came out with the score tied, 3-3, but the Mariners scored once in the top of the ninth. Yankees nemesis Jay Buhner went 0-for-5 at the plate but killed his old team in the field. With two out and one on in the bottom of the ninth, he crashed into the right-field wall to make a run-saving, game-ending catch. New York lost, 4-3, and Abbott was handed another no decision.

In his last start before the All-Star break, against Oakland, Abbott pitched better than he had in quite a while. In nine innings he allowed five hits and two walks, struck out six—his highest number in nearly two months—and retired the last 13 batters he faced. Unfortunately, he also yielded four runs. Meanwhile, New York had the tying run at the plate in each of the last four innings but could score only twice, so Abbott was stuck with a tough loss.

Abbott went into the All-Star break with a record of 7-6. He had lost four and won only one of his past eight starts, and, during that span, his ERA was 5.18, nearly double what it had been through his first 10 outings of the year (2.67). Oddly enough, his control seemed to have improved—his strikeout-to-walk ratio for this stretch was an apparently strong 2.70. However, despite walking just 10 batters in 57⅓ innings, Abbott allowed 65 hits, including 10 home runs, in that same span. His pitches were finding the strike zone, but opposing batters were turning them into hits, not outs.

When the schedule resumed after the All-Star Game, the Yankees set out on a crucial 11-game West Coast road trip. They had closed the first half with a disappointing 3-7 home stand against these same teams (Seattle, Oakland, and California). New York—50-35 at the break—had held first place in the American League East ever since Abbott's victory over Cleveland on May 9, but their lead over the second-place Orioles had shrunk to a mere half game.

Abbott pitched the second-half opener in Seattle and struggled through his worst outing of the year. He lasted just four and two-thirds innings, allowing seven runs on 10 hits—including eight doubles and a home run—and left the game behind, 7-1. However, the Yankees hung tough and, thanks to a seven-run ninth inning, finished on top, 13-8. They went on to sweep the series from the Mariners, scoring runs in large numbers and big bunches—10-8, 9-3, and 14-4.

New York won the first game in Oakland, 5-3, extending the winning streak to five. Abbott took his next turn on the mound, but again he was ineffective. In four of his six innings, he allowed the leadoff hitter to reach base, and three of those times the runner came around to score. All that, combined with Mark McGwire's tape-measure, three-run homer, put Abbott behind, 6-0, and he ended up losing, 6-2. In his last 10 starts, he had won only once and lost five times.

The Yankees took the series closer from Oakland, 1-0, on a superb pitching performance by Melido Perez. The following day they arrived in Anaheim and resumed their high-scoring ways, beating the Angels 11-7, 12-3, and 7-2. Abbott, the ex-Angel, was slated to pitch the final game of the road trip, and it would be a sad return.

On July 13, the day after the All-Star Game, Abbott's good friend and longtime Angels coach Jimmie Reese died at the age of 89. Reese began his 78-year baseball career in 1917 as a batboy for the Los Angeles Angels of the Pacific Coast League. A second baseman, he played for 13 years in the PCL, and later coached and managed in the minors. Reese also played three seasons in the majors (1930–32), the first two with the Yankees, where he was Babe Ruth's roommate, and the other with the St. Louis Cardinals.

For his start against the Angels, Abbott had planned to wear an arm band in honor of his late friend. League rules, however, do not allow that kind of deviation from the official team uniform. Instead, he simply wrote "50," Reese's uniform number when he was a coach with the Angels, on the back of his cap.

As if Reese's death was not enough to upset him, Abbott also lost another one of his best friends. Three days earlier, his dog, Lincoln, was hit by a car and killed outside Abbott's Greenwich, Connecticut, home. To help cheer Abbott up, pitching coach Billy Connors gave him a spaniel puppy.

In the game, Abbott worked eight innings, giving up four runs on seven hits (three of them home runs) and three walks, striking out six. New York came up in the top of the ninth, down 4-2. Angels starter Mark Langston pitched well through eight innings, striking out 10. After a leadoff pop out in the ninth, however, he yielded a single and a walk. Langston seemed tired—he had thrown a total of 144 pitches—so Angels manager Marcel Lachemann brought in right-handed reliever

Joe Grahe. Showalter countered by sending in lefty Don Mattingly to pinch hit.

The night before, Mattingly collected his 2,000th career hit, and for that accomplishment—and because Langston eats left-handed batters for lunch—he was given a well-deserved rest. But with a right-hander now on the mound for California, and two runners on, this looked like the perfect time for hit number 2,001. Mattingly worked the count to two balls and two strikes, and slammed Grahe's next pitch over the 362-foot sign in right field, for a go-ahead, three-run homer. The Yankees bench erupted and Abbott ran down the dugout runway with glee.

Wade Boggs, also resting that day, came in to pinch hit and was hit by a pitch, stole second—only his second stolen base all year—and scored an insurance run on Pat Kelly's single. Steve Howe needed just five pitches to retire the Angels 1-2-3 in the ninth, saving the 6-4 win for Abbott. "I couldn't believe it," Abbott said after the game, reflecting on his narrow escape.

And so, the road trip ended on an amazing high. The Yankees won 10 out of 11 and returned to the Bronx with the best record in baseball (60-36) and a firm, five-and-a-half-game hold on first place. Over this amazing stretch, they scored an average of 8.18 runs per game, the team batting average was a terrific .315, and they hit 30 doubles, four triples, and 19 home runs. Late-inning rallies and come-from-behind wins became almost routine.

"It was exciting," Mike Gallego commented about Mattingly's game-winner in the final game of the trip, "but in a way, I thought, 'OK, it's about time.' That's the feeling you get in this locker room. 'Who's going to be the hero today?'" That's also the feeling you get, he might have added, when you know you're on a winning team.

But although the Yankees were playing great baseball,

as a team, they seemed to lack personality. In the late 1970s, the Yankees were as famous for their fire and emotion—not to mention turmoil—as they were for winning games. Compared with them, the 1994 edition was downright bland. Jim Abbott was no Catfish Hunter, Don Mattingly was no Thurman Munson, Paul O'Neill certainly was no Reggie Jackson, and, thankfully, Buck Showalter was no Billy Martin.

But when Abbott faced Cleveland at Yankee Stadium in late July, the game was marked by some surprising displays of emotion, particularly from Abbott himself. In the second inning, he had a 2-2 count on Albert Belle. Belle took the next pitch, a breaking ball down and in, and Abbott was sure he had struck out the hot batter. However, home-plate umpire Ed Hickox called the pitch a ball. Belle singled on Abbott's next pitch and eventually scored. After the inning, Abbott, from the dugout, berated Hickox about the close call that cost him a run.

The Yankees went ahead, 3-1, in the second and held a 4-2 lead in the bottom of the fifth. But in the top of the sixth, Abbott surrendered solo homers to Belle and—who else?—Manny Ramirez, knotting the score. Showalter, making his second trip to the mound that inning, took the ball from Abbott and handed it to reliever Joe Ausanio.

Still angry about Hickox's ball-three call in the second inning, Abbott stood in the dugout, yelling at the umpire. Then suddenly, he removed the wad of gum from his mouth and threw it the direction of home plate. Afterward, Abbott was reluctant to talk about his unusual and somewhat refreshing public outburst. "C'mon," he chided the reporters, "there's a lot more positive things to focus on in this game."

The two most positive things happened in the bottom of the inning: New York broke the 4-4 tie and Paul O'Neill broke out of an 0-for-21 slump, the worst of his career. His two-out double drove in the run that ultimately kept the Yankees on top, 6-5, and gave them the win. (Two innings later, O'Neill, who is normally even more placid than Abbott, let off a rare eruption of his own, smashing his helmet to the ground after Cleveland's Kenny Lofton robbed him of what seemed to be a sure double in left-center field.)

Abbott gave up eight hits and one walk, striking out four, in five and two-thirds innings, a decent outing. Unfortunately, he again was stung by the long ball, so Showalter pulled him, a bit earlier than Abbott expected. "I was a little surprised," he admitted about the early hook, "but it worked out well. With that August 12 date looming over our heads, maybe you'll see some things done a little more quickly."

August 12. In late July, the players' union had voted that, unless an agreement could be reached by that date, its membership would go on strike. The owners nearly provoked a walkout even earlier when, on August 1, they refused to make a $7.8 million payment into the Players Association health and pension fund. They maintained that, since their four-year benefit agreement with the union had expired on March 19, the teams were under no obligation to contribute to the fund.

However, the union insisted that, even though the agreement had expired, the money was due because its members played in the All-Star Game on July 12, which in past years was a condition of the payment. Reacting to what they perceived as an act of bad faith by the owners, players on at least four teams voted to move the strike date up to August 5. After much discussion, cooler heads prevailed, and the union stuck to its original August 12 deadline.

But now one point was abundantly clear: the owners actually wanted a strike and would provoke one if they could. A long walkout, they hoped, would break the players' union and shift the balance of power back to them. Once that happened, nuisances like free agency and salary arbitration would disappear like bad dreams.

On August 3, a rain-shortened road win over Milwaukee and an Orioles loss secured the American League East crown for the Yankees, should the impending—and now likely—strike end the season in nine days. There was no champagne in the locker room and there would be no ticker-tape parade down Broadway. This was the kind of "victory" that no one cared to celebrate.

The following night, Abbott faced the Twins in what, to some, was an anticlimactic game. But the Yankees, who were 17-3 since the All-Star break, knew they couldn't just play out the string. There could be no letdown, they realized, because maybe the owners would drop their salary-cap demand, maybe the players wouldn't have to strike, maybe the season could go on as usual. And maybe it would snow ice cream in the Sahara Desert.

Abbott worked five and two-thirds innings, giving up two runs on six hits—including a two-run home run by Twins first baseman Kent Hrbek, who announced his retirement that afternoon—and four walks, and striking out five. The Yankees hitters put on a batting clinic, punching out nine runs on 19 hits, including eight doubles and a triple, and Abbott got his ninth win of the season.

What threatened to be Abbott's last start of the season came on August 9, at home against Baltimore. Over 50,000 fans packed the seats for "Phil Rizzuto Night," in honor of the Yankees' ex-shortstop, current broadcaster, and newest inductee into the Baseball Hall of Fame. The celebration had originally been planned for August 13, the day after the strike deadline, but now that the walkout was imminent, it had to be rescheduled.

Abbott pitched about the same as he did against the Twins—six hits, four walks, and four strikeouts in five and two-thirds innings—and for the first time in 12 starts did not give up a home run. (In his 11 previous games he had yielded a total of 17 dingers.) This time, however, the hits and walks clustered for six runs, the Yankees could score no more than five, and Abbott took the 6-5 loss.

Three days later, the major-league baseball players went on strike. Most players expected the walkout, but Abbott, down to the last minute, believed there might be an 11th-hour settlement. "I was planning on this getting worked out," he said, once it became clear that the strike was on, "so I don't even have a plane ticket. I'm still optimistic it might get worked out in a couple of days. If not, I'll go to northern Michigan." It didn't get worked out in a couple of days, or even a couple of weeks, and Abbott headed for his cabin near the lake.

9

≈○ **Unfinished Business**

Negotiations between the owners and the union, when they actually took place, failed to produce any agreement. The players would not accept the salary cap unless, as they previously had requested, the owners furnished proof that their $2 billion-a-year business really needed it. But again, the owners refused to open their books and insisted that the players take their word for it.

Hoping to salvage the season, the Players Association, on September 8, presented an alternative revenue-sharing scheme, one that did not include a salary cap. A day later, management rejected the union's proposal and negotiations broke off. For the baseball owners, it was the salary cap or nothing.

And so, it would be nothing. On September 14, 34 days after the start of the strike, Bud Selig, acting baseball commissioner and owner of the Milwaukee Brewers, announced that 26 of the 28 team owners had voted to cancel the remainder of the 1994 schedule, including the World Series. For the first time since 1969, when divisional play began, there would be no post-season playoffs. For the first time since 1904, when an inter-league squabble derailed the World Series, there would be no Fall Classic.

In all, 669 games, $230 million in players' salaries and $442 million in team revenues, plus an estimated $580 million from the canceled World Series, were lost. Also lost were Frank Thomas's and Albert Belle's bids for the American League Triple Crown, Ken Griffey, Jr.'s, and Matt Williams's chase of Roger Maris's single-season home-run record, and Tony Gwynn's chance to become baseball's first .400 hitter in 53 years. And, for the first time since 1954, Cleveland—one game back in the A.L. Central Division and the leader in the wild-card race—had a real shot to make it into the postseason.

The Yankees ended the truncated schedule with a 70-43 record, first in the American League East by six and one-half games over the Orioles. In all likelihood, the strike cost Don Mattingly his first opportunity in 12-plus years to reach the postseason. The popular Yankees captain had played in 1,657 regular-season games without a postseason appearance, more than any active player except Julio Franco, with 1,658. (Ironically, Franco's team, the Chicago White Sox, was leading the American League Central, and also was on track for postseason play.) At first, Mattingly talked about retiring, but he later promised to be back in Yankees pinstripes whenever baseball resumed.

The strike cost Abbott $788,528 in lost income. It also cost him the chance to get back on track. After an impressive, although somewhat deceptive, beginning (6-2, 2.67 ERA in his first 10 outings), he finished with a 9-8 record and a mediocre 4.55 ERA. (The Yankees hitters supported Abbott well, scoring an average of 5.04 runs in his starts and 6.63 runs in his wins and no decisions.) Although he was one game over .500, the most marginal kind of "winning season," Abbott's 1994 performance was, in many ways, comparable to his 11-14 1993 record.

In his two years with the Yankees, Abbott posted the following numbers:

	IP	H	BB	SO
1993	214	221	73	95
1994	160⅓	167	64	90

Projecting his 1994 statistics over 214 innings (Abbott's 1993 figure) produces the following outcome:

	IP	H	BB	SO
projected 1994	214	223	85	120

Abbott gave up virtually the same amount of hits in both seasons and his strikeout-to-walk ratios were similar (1.41 vs. 1.30). Meanwhile, his strikeouts, after declining for the second straight year in 1993, were back up to his normal level.

But in 1994 Abbott was plagued by two problems: allowing the first batter of the inning to reach base and, even worse, giving up the long ball. Leadoff hitters had a whopping .421 on-base percentage and .494 slugging average against Abbott. When he put the leadoff man on base, the runner scored more than 52 percent of the time. For all of 1993, Abbott allowed 22 home runs, an alarmingly high number at that, but in 1994, he yielded 24 home runs in 53⅔ fewer innings.

So what now? Try as he might, Abbott never felt comfortable playing in New York. For its part, the Yankees front office seemed to lose interest in Abbott once he lost his 90-mile-an-hour fastball. By November, the team began pursuing free-agent pitchers like Bill Swift and Danny Jackson. "We like Jim Abbott," general manager Gene Michael claimed, unconvincingly, "but we're always looking to improve our ballclub. We have to keep all avenues open."

But left-handed pitching is always a scarce commodity. Even though Abbott no longer looked like someone on whom a team would anchor its rotation, plenty of clubs could use an experienced number two or three starter, notably the California Angels. Now that Abbott's old pitching coach and friend, Marcel Lachemann, was managing the team, a return to the site of his first big-league triumphs seemed the most likely—and beneficial—outcome for the left-hander.

In late October, Dave Cunningham, one of Abbott's earliest boosters among the Southern California press, reported in the *Sporting News* that "the Angels are strongly interested in reacquiring pitcher Jim Abbott. If Abbott is granted free agency, signing the Yankees left-hander would probably become the No. 1 priority." But the strike had cast doubt over Abbott's status as a potential free agent.

According to the previous collective bargaining agreement, the 15-day free-agency filing period starts either on the day following the last game of the World Series or, if no Series were played (as in 1994), on October 15. The owners requested a 30-day postponement in filing, but the union balked. And so, on October 15, Jim Abbott was among the first wave of players to declare free agency.

The union insisted that any player who had logged at least six seasons of major-league service, had signed no contract beyond 1994, and had not been a free agent in the past five years could file for free agency. Abbott appeared to meet all these criteria, and his future looked clear. Suddenly, it became clouded.

Abbott began 1994 with five years of big-league service and needed 172 more days—in effect, one full season in the majors—to reach six years. (Although a major-league season actually is 183 days long, with regard to service credit, 172 days counts as one year.) However, the strike ended the 1994 season when it was only 131 days old. The owners' Player Relations Committee, maintaining that Abbott was 41 days short of free-agent eligibility, rejected his bid for free-agent status.

For the next two months, Abbott and the 14 other players who would have qualified for free agency *if not for the strike* seemed stuck in a contractual limbo. Meanwhile, major-league front offices operated on the premise that baseball would resume on schedule in 1995. Managers and general managers were fired and hired, eligible free agents were signed, trades were completed, and ticket prices were raised. And, hoping to polish their tarnished image, the owners took out a full-color, full-page advertisement in the November 8 edition of *USA Today*, pleading their case before the fans.

But instead of improving its public relations, Major League Baseball needed to improve its labor relations. On November 9, after two months of standoff and stalemate, federally appointed mediator William J. Usery finally brought the two sides back to the bargaining table. However, after rounds of proposals and counterproposals, nothing had changed. The owners reasserted their demand for a salary cap, this time in the form of a revenue tax on any club that exceeded 112 percent of the average major-league payroll. The union argued that it was merely a cap in disguise and rejected the notion. Once more, deadlock loomed.

"The clubs cannot remain in limbo as a result of the stalemated negotiations," acting Commissioner Selig announced ominously in early December. "Clubs will make their plans for the 1995 season. . . . There is still time to reach an agreement if the union is serious about negotiating." But in midmonth, talks broke off with little hope of resuming. The owners had gotten what they wanted all along: finally, after repeated threats to do so, they declared an impasse and imposed their rules on the players.

And so, at midnight on December 22, 1994, the Major League Baseball cartel implemented its dreaded salary cap. It also reduced the players' portion of the previous revenue-sharing split from 58 percent to 50 percent, eliminated salary arbitration, and gave restricted free-agent status to players like Abbott, who had four or more big-league seasons, but less than six. If a team wanted to retain one of these players, it would have to make a qualifying offer of at least 110 percent of the player's 1994 salary. The team would then have 10 days to match any other club's offer.

In the meantime, the Yankees, anticipating the impasse, had completed a trade with the White Sox and acquired the bargaining rights to 1993 Cy Young Award winner—and soon-to-be restricted free agent—Jack McDowell. "We'll pursue the player," Gene Michael announced, "and do everything we can to sign the player, within reason." Once the salary cap came into effect, the Yankees would have to tender McDowell a minimum qualifying offer of $5.83 million, and it seemed likely that, after the bidding began, his price tag could rise to $6 million per year for four or five years.

And where did that leave Abbott? In order to retain the left-hander, the Yankees would have had to make him a qualifying offer of $3,052,500 for the 1995 season. But McDowell, and his potentially lofty salary, rendered Abbott's place on the roster superfluous. On December 23, the day after the salary cap was implemented, the Yankees decided not to tender him a qualifying offer. Jim Abbott was now officially an ex-Yankee.

Scott Boras acted as if he were stunned by the Yankees' action. "This may be baseball's answer to Phil Simms," the agent declared. Because of the NFL's salary cap, Simms, a 15-year veteran and still an effective quarterback, was released by the New York Giants shortly before the start of the 1994 football season. "You're letting a premium player go for reasons of the cap," Boras went on, "but not for reasons of the betterment of the team."

Hyperbole is an agent's stock-in-trade. It's his job to exaggerate the value of his client. But after two frustrating years in New York, and a cumulative 20-22 record, it was brutally clear that the only thing "premium" about Boras's client was his $2.775 million contract. The Yankees almost certainly had planned to cut Abbott loose after the 1994 season, salary cap or no salary cap.

"We like Jim," responded an unnamed Yankee official, repeating the organization's official line on Abbott. "But not at the money he's making. It's not a cap thing. We'd just rather spend that money elsewhere." Most likely, the team would spend it on a new pitcher, while Abbott moved on, perhaps back to California, possibly to Detroit, Toronto, or Boston, all of whom appeared to be interested in him for the 1995 season—*if* there were a 1995 season.

"What happened to baseball [in 1994]," mused *New York Newsday* columnist Mike Lupica the day after the salary cap was implemented, "was the worst thing to happen in baseball since the Black Sox scandal of 1919." Baseball's most desperate year drew to a melancholy close amidst continued doubt, and precious little hope, for the coming season. Even worse, the situation had the potential to turn truly ugly.

The owners promised to open the training camps in February, if necessary with so-called replacement players— washed-up has-beens and third-rate pretenders, scabs by another name. Of course, any major leaguers who could be induced to break ranks with their teammates and abandon their brethren also would be welcome. But while management threatened and schemed, the players, led by some of the game's biggest stars, reaffirmed their solidarity and vowed not to cross the picket lines.

So long as the players' union held solid and the owners' cartel remained intransigent, the game of baseball, and Jim Abbott along with it, would stay mired in unfinished business and unanswered questions. But wherever he would play and however he would perform once normal baseball finally resumed, nothing could erase or diminish all that Abbott had already accomplished in his career. His record may not be etched in stone, but it is printed in black and white and, as Casey Stengel used to say, "You could look it up."

What you can't look up, because it can't be expressed in a box score or a record book, is the way that Abbott overcame disability to achieve his dream of pitching in the major leagues. He doesn't want any medals for it. In his own mind, he is just another big-league ballplayer, one who has had both good and bad years, pitched great games and miserable ones, often thrilled the fans and occasionally disappointed them.

In the minds of the public, of course, Abbott is much more. He has become a role model, however reluctantly, to the disabled, and been an inspiration, although unintentionally, to everyone else. Whatever else he hopes to achieve or is able to attain, either on the baseball field or in the wider world, Jim Abbott has nothing left to prove.

⌒o Notes on Sources

I No-Hitter

4   "This ain't a football game": Thomas Boswell, *How Life Imitates the World Series* (New York: Penguin Books, 1983), p. 5.

5   "Why'd you come back?": Tom Verducci, "A Special Delivery," *Sports Illustrated*, September 9, 1993, p. 63.

6   "Let's work the outside": *ibid.*

7   On July 1, 1990, in Chicago, Yankees pitcher Andy Hawkins held the White Sox hitless for eight innings. However, in the bottom of the eighth, Chicago scored four runs on two walks and three Yankees errors to take a 4-0 lead. The Yankees could not score in the top of the ninth, and so the White Sox, as the home team, did not have to bat again. At the time, Hawkins, although the losing pitcher, was credited with a no-hitter. Major-league rules now stipulate that a pitcher must work a complete game of at least *nine* innings to receive credit for a

no-hitter. Consequently, Hawkins's hitless eight-inning complete game is no longer regarded as an official no-hitter.

8 "It puts more pressure on": Jennifer Frey, "Rules of a No-Hitter: No Talking, No Mistakes," *New York Times*, September 5, 1993, sec. 8, p. 3.

9 "Great play": George Vecsey, "The Leather That Saved a No-Hitter," *New York Times*, September 5, 1993, sec. 8, p. 1.

10 "Watch how quickly that phone rings": Jennifer Frey, "Sorry We're Not Here, We're Out Celebrating," *New York Times*, September 6, 1993, p. B27.

10 "I said, 'Come on, feet!' ": Frey, "Rules of a No-Hitter."

10 "The last couple innings": Verducci, p. 62.

11 "You try not to get caught": Frey, "Rules of a No-Hitter."

11 "I didn't know if it was": Vecsey, "The Leather That Saved."

12 "You never want to get no-hit": Jennifer Frey, "Abbott: Not a Hit, Not a Run, Not a Doubt," *New York Times*, September 5, 1993, sec. 8, p. 3.

12 "You always want the ball": Frey, "Rules of a No-Hitter."

12 "I really wanted the ball": *ibid.*

12 "This was Jim Abbott's day": Frey, "Abbott: Not a Hit."

12 "I'm thrilled to come out": *ibid.*, pp. 1, 3.

13 "To be honest": *ibid.*, p. 3.

14 "I have to act like it": Jack Curry, "Abbott Can't Afford to Look Back in Pleasure," *New York Times*, September 10, 1993, p. B11.

14 "If you took every no-hitter": Verducci, p. 62.

15 On September 13, 1883, Hugh Daily, who lost his left hand in a childhood accident, pitched a no-hitter for the Cleveland Spiders of the National League. At that time, the rules of baseball were very different and greatly favored the pitchers. For example, it took seven balls to walk a hitter, and the distance between the pitcher's "box" and home plate was just 50 feet.

2 Dreams

16 "Growing up, I always pictured myself": Tom Callahan, "Dreaming the Big Dreams," *Time*, March 20, 1989, p. 78.

17 "They were young": Ira Berkow, "A Most Extraordinary Fella," *New York Times*, December 12, 1992, p. B7.

17　"All we did is let him": Randy Harvey, "Abbott Prefers Good Arm Is Seen," *Los Angeles Times*, August 17, 1987, sec. 3, p. 12.

17　"The doctor told us": *ibid.*

18　"The only sport Jim didn't need": *ibid.*

18　"When I was little": Mike Penner, "Beyond Success," *Los Angeles Times*, June 1, 1989, sec. 3, p. 10.

19　"Everyone has limitations": Harvey, "Abbott Prefers Good Arm," p. 12.

20　"I still have friends": Penner, "Beyond Success," p. 10.

20　"that's what kids did": Jim Murray, "Positively, Jim Abbott Can Pitch," *Los Angeles Times*, May 31, 1992, p. C9.

21　"We hadn't been paying much attention": Harvey, "Abbott Prefers Good Arm," p. 12.

21　"I was just as curious": *ibid.*

22　"If they think they can bunt": Mike Downey, "This Left-Hander Takes the Right Approach to Life," *Los Angeles Times*, March 17, 1986, sec. 3, p. 11.

22　Holec told *Sports Illustrated*: Hank Hersch, "That Great Abbott Switch," *Sports Illustrated*, May 25, 1987, p. 29.

23　"When Jim pitched": Danny Knobler, "Jim Abbott: Too Good to Be True?" *Baseball America*, June 10, 1988, p. 3.

23　"I honestly feel he is": Harvey, "Abbott Prefers Good Arm," p. 12.

24　"We felt, even at the time": Dave Nightingale, "Abbott Overlooks His Handicap," *Sporting News* (Summer Olympics Special), September 11, 1988, p. 32.

24　"I've grown up daydreaming about pitching": Downey, "This Left-Hander."

24　"The Blue Jays say they didn't": *ibid.*

25　"We've been very cautious": Harvey, "Abbott Prefers Good Arm," p. 12.

25　"I wouldn't have recruited him": *ibid.*

26　"I always felt I could": Nightingale, "Abbott Overlooks His Handicap."

26　"Not only my mom and dad": Downey, "This Left-Hander."

26　"I never heard Jim ask": Berkow, "A Most Extraordinary Fella," p. B7.

3   College Star, Olympic Hero

28   "There's so much attention on him": Mike Downey, "This Left-Hander Takes the Right Approach to Life," *Los Angeles Times*, March 17, 1986, sec. 3, p. 11.

29   "If they had done that": Hank Hersch, "That Great Abbott Switch," *Sports Illustrated*, May 25, 1987, p. 28.

31   "I was amazed that he": Malcolm Moran, "Making the Unusual Routine," *New York Times*, May 23, 1987, sec. 1, p. 48.

32   The scouts examined Abbott closely: Hersch, "That Great Abbott Switch," p. 28.

32   "If you see him pitch": Harvey, "Abbott Prefers Good Arm Is Seen," *Los Angeles Times*, August 17, 1987, sec. 3, p. 12.

32   "They are the best amateur team": George Vecsey, "Abbott Up Front at Games," *New York Times*, August 9, 1987, sec. 5, p. 1.

33   "It was a bang-bang play": Ross Atkin, "Many Pan Am Athletes Get Financial Rewards; Abbott an Inspiration," *Christian Science Monitor*, August 17, 1987, p. 20.

33   "I don't think they took": Harvey, "Abbott Prefers," p. 12.

33   "Abbott's a national hero down there": *ibid.*

33   "It was a great honor": Vecsey, "Abbott Up Front," p. 5.

34   "They've both got a sort of": Harvey, "Abbott Prefers," p. 12.

34   "I was really anxious": Randy Harvey, "US Puts Nicaragua to Rout by 18-0," *Los Angeles Times*, August 13, 1987, sec. 3, p. 8.

34   "The way I look at it": Harvey, "Abbott Prefers," p. 12.

36   "The general public watches him": *ibid.*

36   "the one thing you worry about": *ibid.*

36   "I don't even think about it": *ibid.*

37   "I was sort of shocked": Danny Knobler, "USBF Honor Shocks Abbott," *Baseball America*, November 1987, p. 30.

37   "I had no business being invited": Dave Anderson, "A Natural for the Game," *New York Times*, September 19, 1988, p. C11.

37   "It's just incredible": "Abbott Wins Sullivan," *New York Times*, March 8, 1988, p. A28.

38   "I had a rocky season": D. Anderson, "A Natural."

38   "We decided he was the best": Allen Simpson, "Draft Goes According to Form," *Baseball America*, July 10, 1988, p. 12.

39   "He's actually more suited to": *ibid.*
39   "We looked more closely": *ibid.*
39   "the comebacker is a tough play": D. Anderson, "A Natural."
39   "I guess they didn't know": *ibid.*
40   "It was grueling": Mike Penner, "Beyond Success," *Los Angeles Times*, June 1, 1989, sec. 3, p. 10.
41   "The Japanese are smart players": D. Anderson, "A Natural."
41   "My picture was in the paper": Penner, "Beyond Success," p. 10.
42   "You go down to eat": Scott Ostler, "Budding Young Athlete Has Special Feeling for Abbott," *Los Angeles Times*, September 26, 1988, sec. 3, p. 6.
43   "People see me do that": *ibid.*
44   "It was very close": Mike Downey, "On One Wing and a Prayer . . . US and Abbott Soar to Gold," *Los Angeles Times*, September 29, 1988, sec. 3, p. 4.
45   "I was right on the bottom": *ibid.*
45   "It's a heck of a way": *ibid.*
45   "the best decision I've ever made": *ibid.*
45   "I always thought I would": John Weyler, "Abbott Was Sure He'd Play as a Pro," *Los Angeles Times*, June 2, 1988, sec. 3, p. 1.

4   Rookie

49   "I think it would be": Mike Downey, "Rader Is Ready for Baseball," *Los Angeles Times*, January 24, 1989, sec. 3, p. 1.
50   "has almost as much to do": Mike Penner, "Nothing Throws Jim Abbott," *Los Angeles Times*, March 4, 1989, sec. 3, p. 6.
50   "the first guy I ever faced": Tom Callahan, "Dreaming the Big Dreams," *Time*, March 20, 1989.
50   "There it is": Hank Hersch, "Ace of the Angels," *Sports Illustrated*, September 9, 1991, p. 29.
50   "He probably has as strong": Callahan.
50   Bullpen coach Joe Coleman had: Dave Anderson, "Jim Abbott: Baseball's Real Phenom," *New York Times*, March 9, 1989, p. D27.
51   "Everybody's in the dugout going": Penner, "Nothing Throws Jim Abbott," p. 6.

52   "How about that first batter?": *ibid.*

52   "I've been doing this since": *ibid.*

52   "He was trying to overthrow": Scott Ostler, "A Budding Abbott Is Spring Discovery," *Los Angeles Times,* March 9, 1989, sec. 3, p. 3.

52   "Those were our initial plans": Mike Penner, "Abbott Delivers Message with Strikeout of Canseco," *Los Angeles Times,* March 8, 1989, sec. 3, p. 3.

53   "I think Abbie is the kind": Ostler, "A Budding Abbott."

53   "The other day against Oakland": Mike Penner, "Another Impressive Showing by Abbott," *Los Angeles Times,* March 12, 1989, sec. 3, p. 10.

53   "If this keeps up much longer": *ibid.*

54   "I don't think anybody comes": *ibid.*

54   "Jim deserves to be": John Weyler, "Abbott's Spot on Team Appears Safe," *Los Angeles Times,* March 28, 1989, sec. 3, pp. 1, 4.

55   "Historically, there's been a tendency": Tom Singer, "Bichette Gets Reprieve," *Sporting News,* March 27, 1989, p. 28.

55   "But then I realized": Dave Nightingale, "Abbott's in Rotation," *Sporting News,* April 3, 1989.

56   "I've slowly been brought around": *ibid.*

56   "Abbott has three things": John Weyler, "It's Official, Abbott Will Be Fifth Starter," *Los Angeles Times,* March 30, 1989, sec. 3, p. 7.

57   "There was definitely some nervousness": John Weyler, "Abbott Cheered, Before and After," *Los Angeles Times,* April 9, 1989, sec. 3, p. 6.

57   "I thought the pitch": *ibid.*

57   "I did what I wanted": *ibid.*

57   "That was one ovation": Tom Singer, "Abbott Handles Media, But Not M's," *Sporting News,* April 17, 1989, p. 24.

58   "Under the conditions, I thought": Mike Penner, "Angels' 7-0 Defeat Pinned on Abbott, Not All the Blame," *Los Angeles Times,* sec. 3, p. 6.

58   "I don't think I threw": *ibid.*

58   "I was surprised at how hard": Weyler, "Abbott Cheered, Before and After."

59   "I wasn't contributing": John Weyler, "Jim Abbott Gets His First Win," *Los Angeles Times*, April 25, 1989, sec. 3, p. 1.

60   "I jumped up and down": *ibid.*, p. 8.

60   "If the team doctor hadn't": Tom Singer, "Abbott Sweats Out a Juicy Victory," *Sporting News*, May 8, 1989, p. 22.

60   "Vindication is not the right word": Weyler, "Jim Abbott Gets His," p. 8.

60   "Now I feel more and more": Singer, "Abbott Sweats Out."

61   "Some days it seems like": Scott Ostler, "Rookie's Hope: To Be Merely Another Angel," *Los Angeles Times*, June 1, 1989, sec. 3, p. 1.

61   "He used to say": Jim Bouton, *Ball Four* (New York: The World Publishing Company, 1970), p. 74.

61   "I had the most": Rob Brofman, "One for the Angels," *Life*, June 1989, p. 120.

61   "if a pitcher doesn't do well": Bouton, pp. 74–75.

61   "When you've pitched and done poorly": Brofman, p. 120.

61   "marvels at the vets": Ostler, "Rookie's Hope," p. 10.

62   "This was certainly a longtime dream": Mike Penner, "Dream Almost as Abbott Imagined," *Los Angeles Times*, June 18, 1989, sec. 3, p. 8.

62   "I just tried to have him": *ibid.*

63   "He got just two balls up": *ibid.*

63   "I don't think I want to": *ibid.*

63   "His capacity to learn": John Weyler, "Abbott Gets More Than a Win," *Los Angeles Times*, July 9, 1989, sec. 3, p. 8.

64   "He was as upset as": *ibid.*, p. 1.

64   "I gave up too many hits": *ibid.*

65   "Actually I'm kinda disgusted": Tom Singer, "A.L. West: Angels," *Sporting News*, August 14, 1989, p. 17.

65   "Now there's one record": Tom Singer, "Win No. 7 Gives Abbott a Record," *Sporting News*, July 17, 1989, p. 26.

66   "All the questions about him": Peter Gammons, "No More Doubts," *Sports Illustrated*, July 24, 1989, p. 65.

5   A Reluctant Role Model

68   "You don't have to ask": Bruce Anderson, "Angel on the Ascent," *Sports Illustrated*, March 13, 1989, p. 27.

68   "He is the Rookie of Spring": Scott Ostler, "A Budding Abbott Is Spring Discovery," *Los Angeles Times*, March 9, 1989, sec. 3, p. 3.

69   Marcel Lachemann wondered: B. Anderson, "Angel on the Ascent."

69   "Jim has received more attention": Mike Penner, "Beyond Success," *Los Angeles Times*, June 1, 1989, sec. 3, p. 10.

70   "You're my hero": John Weyler, "Abbott Gets More Than a Win," *Los Angeles Times*, July 9, 1989, sec. 3, p. 8.

70   "This is incredible": Peter Gammons, "No More Doubts," *Sports Illustrated*, July 24, 1989, p. 64.

70   "I think of something": Art Spander, "Let's Appreciate What Abbott Does Have," *Sporting News*, March 13, 1989, p. 6.

70   "All the attention has been encouraging": Tom Singer, "Abbott's Attention on Proving He's Real," *Sporting News*, March 13, 1989, p. 31.

71   "But that would constitute": *ibid*.

71   "He may be the most remarkable": Gammons, "No More Doubts," p. 64.

71   "Theirs is a different culture": Penner, "Beyond Success," p. 10.

71   And some questions set: *ibid*.

72   "we'd also have a 50-year-old pitcher": *ibid*.

72   "Pete Gray lost his arm": Dave Anderson, "Jim Abbott: Baseball's Real Phenom," *New York Times*, March 9, 1989, p. D27.

72   "I never told myself": Tom Callahan, "Dreaming the Big Dreams," *Time*, March 20, 1989, p. 78.

73   "The boys and girls": Scott Ostler, "Rookie's Hope To Be Merely Another Angel," *Los Angeles Times*, June 1, 1989, sec. 3, p. 10.

73   "When talk shifts from the left": Hank Hersch, "That Great Abbott Switch," *Sports Illustrated*, May 25, 1987, p. 28.

73   "and [he] tightens it nervously": Charles Leerhsen, with Tim Padgett, "The Complete Jim Abbott," *Newsweek*, June 12, 1989, p. 60.

73   "If I had two hands": Penner, "Beyond Success," p. 10.

73   to Randy Sobek: Scott Ostler, "Budding Young Athlete Has Special Feeling for Abbott," *Los Angeles Times*, September 26, 1988, sec. 3, p. 6.

74   to Erin Bower: Jim Murray, "Not Only Does He Understand, He Shows He Cares," *Los Angeles Times*, July 18, 1989, sec. 3, pp. 1, 4.

74   to Laura Small: Eric Lichtblau, "Abbott Helps Kids Explore Potential of Inner Strength," *Los Angeles Times*, August 4, 1989, sec. 3, p. 8.

75   "I pitch to win": John Weyler, "Abbott Was Sure He'd Play as a Pro," *Los Angeles Times*, June 2, 1988, sec. 3, p. 10.

75   "I saw Abbott pitch three times": Bill James, *The Baseball Book 1990* (New York: Villard Books, 1990), p. 169.

75   Abbott described for *Sports Illustrated*: Hank Hersch, "Ace of the Angels," *Sports Illustrated*, September 9, 1991, p. 29.

76   "For the first time": *ibid.*

76   "I think it's my parents": Ira Berkow, "A Most Extraordinary Fella," *New York Times*, December 12, 1992, p. B9.

76   "I can only imagine what": Penner, "Beyond Success," p. 10.

77   "When people talk of me": *ibid.*

77   "Jim is the most *un*handicapped person": Leerhsen.

6   Downs and Ups

79   "I am shocked": "$185,00 for Abbott Has Agent Seething," *Sporting News*, March 26, 1990, p. 32.

79   "I really enjoy the camaraderie here": Helene Elliott, "Abbott Was Event; Now He's a Pitcher," *Los Angeles Times*, March 28, 1990, p. C8.

81   "I think the team's mood": "Rader: Club Between Asleep and Frantic," *Sporting News*, August 6, 1990, p. 11.

82   Pitching coach Marcel Lachemann thus felt: Hank Hersch, "Ace of the Angels," *Sports Illustrated*, September 9, 1991, p. 24.

82   "I think I've had a better": Helene Elliott, "Let the Record Show That Abbott Was Better," *Los Angeles Times*, September 27, 1990, p. C4.

83   "Instead of just pitching to people": *ibid.*, p. C5.

83   "Could I win 20 games?": *ibid.*

84   "He will suggest": Hersch, "Ace of the Angels," p. 29.

84   "I'm too big to cry": Dave Cunningham, "A.L. West: California Angels," *Sporting News*, May 6, 1991, p. 24.

85   "It was all about pitching": Hersch, "Ace of the Angels," p. 22.

85   "I told him": Helene Elliott, "Drought Finally Over for Abbott," *Los Angeles Times*, May 6, 1991, pp. C1, C7.

85   "It was the toughest thing": Hersch, "Ace of the Angels," p. 24.

86   "If we score six runs": Elliott, "Drought Finally Over," p. C7.

86   "I may steal it": *ibid.*

86   "Several times I've seen him": Hersch, "Ace of the Angels," pp. 22–23.

87   "Last year, he was one-dimensional": Dave Cunningham, "A.L. West: California Angels," *Sporting News*, August 26, 1991, p. 23.

87   "It's ridiculous": Dave Cunningham, "A.L. West: California Angels," *Sporting News*, October 7, 1991, p. 26.

87   Author Bill James evaluates: Bill James, *The Bill James Baseball Abstract 1988* (New York: Ballantine Books, 1988), pp. 31–33.

88   James went on to develop: *ibid.*, pp. 159–160.

88   James figured that, in 1991: Bill James, *The Baseball Book 1992* (New York: Villard Books, 1992), p. 59.

89   "A loss is a loss": Helene Elliott, "Borders Turns Odds Against Angels," *Los Angeles Times*, September 25, 1991, p. C4.

90   "We have the nucleus": Dave Cunningham, "A.L. West: California Angels," *Sporting News*, September 16, 1991, p. 25.

90   "We scored only two runs": Dave Nightingale, "Hold On, Cowboy!" *Sporting News*, December 23, 1991, p. 21.

91   "The Cowboy has waited 30 years": *ibid.*

92   "Without arbitration": Whitey Herzog, "When Owners Gave Arbitration, They Sold the House," *Sporting News*, February 24, 1992, p. 8.

92   "If the Angels want me around": Helene Elliott, "Abbott Agrees to $1.85 Million," *Los Angeles Times*, March 17, 1992, p. C7.

93   "You can pitch very well": Helene Elliott, "Triumvirate Rules Mound," *Los Angeles Times*, March 17, 1992, p. C5.

93   Jackie Autry met with reporters: Dave Cunningham, "All Talk,

No Action on the Trade Front," *Sporting News*, April 6, 1992, p. S-30.

94   "We can't hit": Dave Nightingale, "No Repeat Business," *Sporting News*, April 6, 1992, p. S-12.

94   "This is the toughest game": Helene Elliott, "Abbott Finds No Solace in 1-0 Loss," *Los Angeles Times*, April 30, 1992, p. C6.

95   "I have to find rewards": "No Runs, No Fun," *Sporting News*, June 8, 1992, p. 16.

95   "We know we're playing bad baseball": Dave Cunningham, "A.L. West: California Angels," *Sporting News*, June 15, 1992, p. 38.

95   "You know it hurts": Dave Cunningham, "A.L. West: California Angels," *Sporting News*, July 13, 1992, p. 26.

96   "We're not going to trade Abbott": Dave Cunningham, "A.L. West: California Angels," *Sporting News*, August 10, 1992, p. 38.

96   "The won-loss record is obviously": Dave Cunningham, "A.L. West: California Angels," *Sporting News*, August 31, 1992, p. 29.

96   "I guess you could say": *ibid.*

96   "It seems like every time": Dave Cunningham, "A.L. West: California Angels," *Sporting News*, September 7, 1992, p. 27.

97   Bill James devised a series: Bill James, *The Bill James Baseball Abstract 1984* (New York: Ballantine Books, 1984), pp. 229–230.

98   "Have you heard?": Mike Downey, "Abbott Goes to Work in a Pin-Striped Suit," *Los Angeles Times*, February 10, 1993, pp, C1, C10.

7   Yankee

99   "This is my deal": Helene Elliott, "Yankees Get Abbott for Minor Leaguers," *Los Angeles Times*, December 7, 1992, p. C13.

99   "I'd talked to [Yankees general manager]": Joe Sexton, "Yanks Are Winners in Abbott Derby," *New York Times*, December 7, 1992, p. C3.

100   "It boiled down to waiting": Elliott, "Yankees Get Abbott," p. C13.

101   "knows that the best way": Dave Cunningham, "A.L. West: California Angels," *Sporting News,* November 21, 1994, p. 42.

101   "It's sad that this has come": Elliott, "Yankees Get Abbott," p. C13.

101   "We're going to take heat": Dave Cunningham, "A.L. West: California Angels," *Sporting News,* December 21, 1992, p. 32.

102   "a pitcher with a proven record": Ross Newhan, "When the Bottom Line Becomes Goal, Fans Suffer," *Los Angeles Times,* December 7, 1992, p. C1.

102   "I have never enjoyed watching": Mike Downey, "Abbott Goes to Work in a Pin-Striped Suit," *Los Angeles Times,* February 10, 1993, p. C10.

102   "It's been a tough day": Joe Sexton, "Shocked, Stunned, Adjusting to Deal," *New York Times,* December 8, 1992, p. B19.

103   "When Bryan Harvey left": Dave Cunningham, "A.L. West: California Angels," *Sporting News,* January 11, 1993, p. 33.

103   "The pinstripes, the tradition": Jack O'Connell, "A.L. East: New York Yankees," *Sporting News,* December 28, 1992, p. 40.

104   "Hey, I'm a Michigan boy": Downey, "Abbott Goes to Work," p. C1.

104   "a Californian through and through": *ibid.*, p. C10.

104   "We want to experience the city": *ibid.*

104   General manager Gene Michael has said: Dave Nightingale, "The Poison Apple," *Sporting News,* March 8, 1993, p. 13.

105   "How many players summon reporters": Jack Curry, "He'll Take Manhattan and a New Contract, Too," *New York Times,* March 27, 1993, p. 31.

105   "New York did bring out": Nightingale, "The Poison Apple," p. 13.

106   "You'll like the fans": Ira Berkow, "A Most Extraordinary Fella," *New York Times,* December 12, 1992, p. B9.

106   "I didn't have the guts": Downey, "Abbott Goes to Work," p. C10.

106   "Everybody talks about New York": Ross Newhan, "The Thrill Isn't All Gone," *Los Angeles Times,* April 27, 1993, p. C5.

106   "George is just like New York": Nightingale, "The Poison Apple," p. 14.

107   "I have no problem": Berkow, "A Most Extraordinary Fella," p. B9.

107 "We're interested in signing him": Jack Curry, "Yankees Consider Lengthy Abbott Deal," *New York Times*, January 5, 1993, p. B9.

108 "I think Jim's view": *ibid.*

108 "They're not in the same category": *ibid.*

108 "I hope there isn't any problem": Murray Chass, "Abbott Gets Ruffled About Arbitration Loss," *New York Times*, February 13, 1993, p. 31.

109 "The Yankees used a very negative": *ibid.*

109 "Why did they trade for me": *ibid.*

109 "It's not easy coming to": Claire Smith, "Abbott Ignoring Arbitration Loss," *New York Times*, February 19, 1993, p. B9.

110 "I think their price was": Chass, "Abbott Gets Ruffled."

110 "While I was comfortable in California": Smith, "Abbott Ignoring," p. B12.

110 "They'll be talking about Jim Abbott": Bob Nightengale, "Specter of Abbott Deal Haunts Opening of Camp," *Los Angeles Times*, February 22, 1993, p. C5.

111 "A lot of people who": *ibid.*

111 "You know what March 1 is": Chass, "Abbott Gets Ruffled."

111 "I'm in the right place": Jack Curry, "Abbott Is Prepared to Wear Out the Pinstripes," *New York Times*, March 11, 1993, p. B19.

112 "could be the most exciting place": Curry, "He'll Take Manhattan."

112 "the ball [is] in their court": Curry, "Abbott Is Prepared."

112 "I'm not involved in any": *ibid.*

112 "I hit over .400": "Abbott Proves a Hit at Bat," *New York Times*, March 9, 1993, p. B12.

113 "Baseball is fun again": Curry, "He'll Take Manhattan."

113 "That was one of the real": Newhan, "The Thrill Isn't," p. C5.

114 "It wasn't as hard as": Bob Nightengale, "Abbott Returns, Will Face Langston," *Los Angeles Times*, April 28, 1994, p. C4.

114 "It's going to be exciting": Newhan, "The Thrill Isn't," p. C5.

114 "It was a nice feeling": Bob Nightengale, "Langston Outduels Abbott," *Los Angeles Times*, April 29, 1993, p. C6.

115 "I really feel bad for Jim": *ibid.*

115 "It's going to take a long": *ibid.*, p. C1.

115 "There were never any negotiations": Jack O'Connell, "A.L. East: New York Yankees," *Sporting News*, May 3, 1993, p. 27.

116 "That guy's a class act": Jack O'Connell, "A.L. East: New York Yankees," *Sporting News*, June 7, 1993, p. 29.

116 "I think the whole world": *ibid.*

118 "It has been a pretty tough": Jack O'Connell and Mark Newman, "Gem, Abbott," *Sporting News*, September 13, 1993, p. 13.

118 "The guys who haven't done": Jack Curry, "Steinbrenner Changes a Muzzle into a Prod," *New York Times*, September 14, 1993, p. B13.

119 "I don't understand the timing": Jack Curry, "Showalter Insists He's Undeterred Amid the Sudden Steinbrenner Tumult," *New York Times*, September 15, 1993, p. B19.

119 "If a player doesn't have courage": Dave Anderson, "The Heart of the Matter," *New York Times*, September 16, 1993, p. B11.

119 "If he singled me out": Curry, "Showalter Insists He's Undeterred."

119 "New York is New York": Curry, "Abbott Can't Afford," pp. B11, B13.

120 "It's not a great season": Jack O'Connell, "A.L. East: New York Yankees," *Sporting News*, September 20, 1993, p. 24.

120 "No, I didn't think about it": Jack Curry, "Yankees Heading Home, Their Heads Bowed," *New York Times*, September 16, 1993, p. B14.

121 "If Melido Perez and Jim Abbott": Jack Curry, "Yanks' Peaks and Valleys of '93," *New York Times*, October 1, 1993, p. B13.

122 "We're talking about a guy": Bob Nightengale, "Is Abbott in Angels' Future?" *Los Angeles Times*, September 23, 1993, p. C4.

8   The Long, Short Season

123 "Once I got away from": Mike Lupica, "He's Tuned for Glory," *New York Daily News*, February 17, 1994, p. 77.

124 "I used to wear that": Jack Curry, "Abbott Hopes That Conquering Passion Will Extinguish Pain," *New York Times*, January 17, 1994, p. C3.

124 "deal with the mental side": *ibid.*

124 "pitched the way we thought": *ibid.*

125 "I'd like to stay here": *ibid.*

125 "by almost all definitions": Jon Heyman, "Abbott's New Pitch," *New York Newsday*, February 17, 1994, p. 182.

126 "no-decision change-ups, where the hitter": Charlie Nobles, "Abbott Stresses Product Over Result," *New York Times*, March 24, 1994, p. B19.

127 "Jim Abbott's got to give": Jon Heyman, "Boss on Abbott: Cut the Charity," *New York Newsday*, February 26, 1994, p. 90.

127 "I don't like to be told": *ibid.*

128 "Jim Abbott just can't say no": Mark Hermann, "All-Star Givers," *New York Newsday/Sports New York*, December 24–25, 1994, p. 10.

128 So are many of his teammates: Jon Heyman, "Odd, Even for the Boss," *New York Newsday/Sports New York*, February 27, 1994, p. 19.

132 "I've worked hard on that": Joe Donnelly, "Best of Abbott," *New York Newsday*, April 9, 1994, p. A38.

133 "It's up to him whether": Jack O'Connell, "A.L. East: New York Yankees," *Sporting News*, April 25, 1994, p. 24.

139 "I'm thrilled for Lach": "A.L. West Notes: California Angels," *USA Today Baseball Weekly*, May 25–31, 1994, p. 13.

140 "It's definitely tough playing in": Jon Heyman, "The Yankees Shift to Cruise Control," *New York Newsday*, May 25, 1994, p. A64.

140 "He tends to shake up": *ibid.*

141 "The rib wrap is limiting": Jon Heyman, "Wrap of Ribs," *New York Newsday*, May 26, 1994, p. A106.

141 "The basic technique is to reduce": "A.L. East Notes: New York Yankees," *USA Today Baseball Weekly*, May 25–31, 1994, p. 11.

147 "I couldn't believe it": Jon Heyman, "Trip to Heaven," *New York Newsday*, July 25, 1994, p. A86.

147 "It was exciting": *ibid.*

148 "C'mon": Jon Heyman, "Yankees Are Hot Stuff," *New York Newsday/Sports New York*, July 31, 1994, p. 3.

149 "I was a little surprised": *ibid.*

151 "I was planning on this": Jon Heyman, "So, Now What?" *New York Newsday*, August 12, 1994, p. A85.

9   Unfinished Business

155   "We like Jim Abbott": Jon Heyman, "Yankees Join Race for Swift," *New York Newsday*, November 15, 1994, p. A74.

155   "the Angels are strongly interested": Dave Cunningham, "A.L. West: California Angels," *Sporting News*, October 31, 1994, p. 56.

157   "The clubs cannot remain in limbo": "Mediator: Don't Impose Cap Now," *New York Newsday*, December 7, 1994, p. A65.

157   "We'll pursue the player": Jon Heyman, "Yankees, McDowell Talk Despite Uncertain Status," *New York Newsday*, December 21, 1994, p. A73.

158   "This may be baseball's answer": Jon Heyman, "Yankees Will Let Abbott Go," *New York Newsday*, December 22, 1994, p. A77.

158   "We like Jim": Jeff Bradley, "Yanks Set to Unload Abbott Today," *New York Daily News*, December 23, 1994, p. 78.

158   "What happened to baseball": Mike Lupica, "Owners' Dastardly Fix Is In," *New York Newsday*, December 23, 1994, p. A63.

⌒○ Index